Essentials of
Qualitative Interviewing

Qualitative Essentials

Series Editor: Janice Morse
University of Utah

Series Editorial Board: H. Russell Bernard, Kathy Charmaz, D. Jean Clandinin, Juliet Corbin, Carmen de la Cuesta, John Engel, Sue E. Estroff, Jane Gilgun, Jeffrey C. Johnson, Carl Mitcham, Katja Mruck, Judith Preissle, Jean J. Schensul, Sally Thorne, John van Maanen, Max van Manen.

Qualitative Essentials is a book series providing a comprehensive but succinct overview of topics in qualitative inquiry. These books fill an important niche in qualitative methods for students—and others new to the qualitative research—who require rapid but complete perspective on specific methods, strategies, and important topics. Written by leaders in qualitative inquiry, alone or in combination, these books are excellent resources for instructors and students from all disciplines. Proposals for the series should be sent to the series editor at explore@lcoastpress.com.

Titles in this series:

1. *Naturalistic Observation*, Michael V. Angrosino
2. *Essentials of Qualitative Inquiry*, Maria J. Mayan
3. *Essentials of Field Relationships*, Amy Kaler and Melanie A. Beres
4. *Essentials of Accessible Grounded Theory*, Phyllis Norerager Stern and Caroline Jane Porr
5. *Essentials of Qualitative Interviewing*, Karin Olson
6. *Essentials of Transdisciplinary Research*, Patricia Leavy

Essentials of
Qualitative Interviewing

Karin Olson

Left Coast
Press Inc.

Walnut Creek, California

LEFT COAST PRESS, INC.
1630 North Main Street, #400
Walnut Creek, CA 94596
http://www.LCoastPress.com

Left Coast Press Inc.

ISBN 978-1-59874-594-8 hardcover
ISBN 978-1-59874-595-5 paperback

green press
INITIATIVE

Left Coast Press is committed to preserving ancient forests and natural resources. We elected to print this title on 30% post consumer recycled paper, processed chlorine free. As a result, for this printing, we have saved:

4 Trees (40' tall and 6-8" diameter)
2 Million BTUs of Total Energy
465 Pounds of Greenhouse Gases
2,097 Gallons of Wastewater
133 Pounds of Solid Waste

Left Coast Press made this paper choice because our printer, Thomson-Shore, Inc., is a member of Green Press Initiative, a nonprofit program dedicated to supporting authors, publishers, and suppliers in their efforts to reduce their use of fiber obtained from endangered forests.

For more information, visit www.greenpressinitiative.org

Environmental impact estimates were made using the Environmental Defense Paper Calculator. For more information visit: www.papercalculator.org.

Printed in the United States of America

♾™ The paper used in this publication meets the minimum requirements of American National Standard for Information Sciences—Permanence of Paper for Printed Library Materials, ANSI/NISO Z39.48–1992.

Contents

To my students, with thanks
for their enthusiasm and interest in interviewing
in the context of qualitative research.

Foreword

Svend Brinkmann, Ph.D., Professor
Director of the Center for Qualitative Studies, Aalborg University, Denmark

In the last couple of decades, interviewing has become a very popular qualitative research method across the human, social, and health sciences. For as long as we know, human beings have used conversation as a central tool for obtaining knowledge about others, how they experience the world, how they think, act, and feel. Obviously, conversation is much more than a neutral tool for obtaining knowledge; it is also a mode of being together for individuals, a distinctive way in which we can share thoughts and emotions, which also means that conversations can harm us if others transgress our zone of intimacy or if we realize things about our lives that we prefer not to know.

Although conversations seem to be at the core of humanity, the qualitative research interview is still relatively new as a formal research method. A significant challenge, when teaching and learning research interviewing, relates to the fact that almost everyone seems capable of doing it, even before they learn about interviewing as a research method. Because of the complexities of conversations and social interactions, this straightforwardness is often illusory, and, if one is not careful, a double risk arises of producing knowledge that is superficial, on the one hand, and of acting in an ethically insensitive way, on the other.

Reading Karin Olson's book on interviewing will prepare newcomers to exercise the craft of qualitative interviewing in a way that is likely to produce significant knowledge on a firm ethical basis. Attention is firmly kept on the fact that the goal of interviewing is to produce knowledge that is useful, but this epistemic dimension is continuously coupled with a sensitive ethical awareness. Olson demonstrates very concretely how to initiate and conclude an interview, how to ask questions, how to transcribe and analyze—even down to the details of coding, writing notes in the margin, and so on. We also learn about the importance of researcher standpoint, questions about how to interview different populations, and the potential of different forms of interviewing (face to face but also phone and email interviews).

There are three general ways of writing about interviewing. The first one presents discrete steps in a research process that should be followed more or less mechanically. The second one rejects all such standardized formats and valorizes individual creativity and intuition. Olson's book is particularly valuable, because it succeeds in striking a balance between these extremes and communicates how to do research based on how she in fact works, what has been helpful in her own research projects, and how her students and colleagues have proceeded. This could be called the third approach, a craft approach to interviewing that enables the reader to look over the shoulder of an experienced researcher, which is very useful to new-comers and also enlightening to more experienced researchers. The clear and accessible style of this book and its many concrete examples, based on many years of work in teaching and practicing qualitative research inter-viewing, will make it a valuable resource for students in qualitative research courses for years to come.

Preface

Interviewing is like making bread; one may be able to describe the process of bread making in detail, based on good examples provided by expert bread makers, but one's knowledge isn't really proved until the bread is made and eaten. This book outlines some of the core principals related to making good interviews in the context of qualitative research and provides the encouragement for success. Just as with bread making, practice improves the product—in this case, the ability to ask the "right" questions gets easier, and the data get better.

This book introduces the beginning qualitative researcher to interviewing and provides those who are already working in this field with reminders about some of the core principles regarding interviewing. I have structured the book around things I wish I had known more about when I began conducting qualitative studies.

I draw on conversations that took place in courses and workshops on interviewing that I taught over the past twenty years, and I am grateful to the many students and colleagues who participated in those conversations. I also incorporate key points currently being discussed in the literature on interviewing and lessons I learned as a qualitative researcher.

I begin with a discussion of standpoint and the importance of situating one's self in one's study. I follow with a chapter on identification of the research participant. Chapter 3 focuses on the various types of interviews used in the course of qualitative studies and approaches to data generation within each of these.

Chapter 4 discusses the logistics of interviewing and provides practical advice about how to address some of the challenges of interviewing.

Chapter 5 covers the process of transforming the interview into data. In this chapter I provide a detailed account of issues related to both recording and transcription, discuss ways to manage the data arising from interviews, and illustrate a simple way to begin coding an interview.

Chapter 6 begins by providing an overview of issues related to consent and then focuses on some of the unique ethical issues related to interviews. In this chapter I also provide a discussion of issues related to the maintenance of boundaries in the interview process.

Chapter 7 summarizes the main points of the book.

I hope this book serves as a springboard for many interesting conversations about interviewing and qualitative research.

Acknowledgments

I am filled with gratitude for the amazing individuals who have been part of this book. I would like to thank Jan Morse for her friendship and for asking me to write this book, Mitch Allen and colleagues from Left Coast Press, Inc., for their support and encouragement, and Moira Calder for her editorial support. I would also like to thank Christine Ceci for our many conversations that helped to shape Chapter 1, Catherine Kubrak for her help in fine-tuning the hypothetical data in Chapter 5, and Maria Mayan for her insights about all things qualitative. These people ensured that the solitary process of writing was not a lonely one.

The time required for writing always takes time from something else, and in my case, it came from time I would have normally spent with my family. Thus I am very grateful to my husband, Brian Mason, our sons, Peter Martin and Alex Mason, our daughter-in-law, Jeanie Tse, and our amazing grandson, Leif Martin, for their love, good humor, and patience, despite my preoccupation with this book over the past months.

I enjoyed the process of writing. One of the best parts, from my point of view, was the time it provided for reflecting on the things I have learned about interviewing and the people who have been part of my journey. I hope this small volume helps new qualitative researchers to build their skills as interviewers and to understand the value of relationships in research.

Karin Olson
Edmonton, Canada
May 2011

I. A Matter of Standpoint

Standpoint is about the "footprints" we leave in a study by virtue of who we are and the research designs we use. I have chosen to begin this book on interviewing in qualitative research with a brief discussion about standpoint, because I think it has a profound influence on the way we think about the data we obtain through interviewing.

The Researcher's Standpoint: Who Are You?

As a researcher, before you begin any study, you must stop and think about how you came to be interested in the topic of study. When did it grab your interest? What things led up to that point in time? Who has influenced your interests? Why is your topic important? What difference will it make that this study is being done by you rather than by some else? How could your gender, age, experiences, and ethnicity influence the way you will analyze the data? These questions all underscore an important principle in qualitative research, which is the idea that the researcher brings a particular standpoint to any study that he or she conducts. Frank (2000) has noted that standpoint "requires self-consciousness about how the fate and choices in your life have positioned you in the world and with whom you have been positioned" (p. 356).

A person's standpoint is neither right nor wrong. It must be identified and acknowledged, however, because whether we realize it or not, it influences all aspects of our studies, beginning with the development of the research question. One way to learn more about your standpoint is to reflect on who you are in relation to the topic you want to study. Do this yourself, or ask a friend or colleague to interview you. What do you bring to this field of study? Why is this topic important to you? What experiences have you had in relation to your research topic? Perhaps you recently became a parent, for example, and are planning to study some aspect of parenting. How will your experience influence your research? What difference would it make if you decided to conduct a study in an area where you had limited experience?

As a person who has taught qualitative research methods to students from various disciplines, I have noticed that one's discipline also influences the topic of study. For example, one student with whom I recently worked, who was from a social work background, wanted to study work-life balance. She quickly realized that one of the assumptions she had made was that work-life balance was both possible and good. As she reflected on her assumptions, however, she began to question them and then to make notes about standpoint. For example, she wondered how the standpoints of employers and employees on work-life balance might differ. She also wondered about differences in the standpoints of men and women and how people's other family responsibilities, such as the care of young children or aging parents, might influence the ways in which they thought about work-life balance. These reflections helped her identify her standpoint about work-life balance and move from her topic of interest to her research question.

Think about work-life balance from the standpoint of your discipline. How might you approach a study of work-life balance? Now shift your thoughts to your discipline more broadly. What are the important questions for a study of work-life balance from the standpoint of your discipline? The point is not to "answer" these questions. You must, however, think about them and track how your thoughts about them change over time. Watch closely as some ideas slip away and new ideas become important in your thinking. See the patterns in your thinking. See yourself becoming a scholar involved in the exciting discovery of new knowledge.

Reflecting on who you are and the assumptions you bring to your study is important, because it will influence the research questions that anchor your study. Make a list of all of the possible research questions related to your topic, and think about your standpoint in relation to each of them. It is impossible to move forward in a study until this step is completed, because the nature of the research question has implications for the choice of research design. It is true that the research question sometimes changes once a study is underway, even to the point of necessitating changes in design. Nevertheless, the time spent firmly anchoring a research question to one's standpoint at the beginning of a project provides a solid foundation for next steps in the research process.

Standpoint and Research Design

Once the topic of interest begins to settle into a research question, the next task of the researcher is to choose the research design that is best suited to the research question. With this decision come two new angles on standpoint related to the assumptions "built into" the design selected: perspective and assumptions about research.

Emic and/or Etic Perspective

The first of these angles is related to whether the researcher would like to study from the perspective of an "insider" (emic) or an "outsider" (etic). The decision about whether to approach a research question from an emic or an etic perspective influences who the research participants will be and how the data will be collected.

An emic perspective is one of the hallmarks of qualitative research (Fetterman, 2008), because the objective is to learn as much as possible about an experience directly from the person who had the experience and who is able to describe it. As a result, the data in a study being conducted from an emic perspective are often collected using interviews. When a study is conducted from an etic perspective, in contrast, the researcher is more likely to use quantitative approaches and to obtain data using validated instruments and other such approaches. In the course of considering the research question, the researcher might realize that data from both emic and etic perspectives are required and as a result would construct his or her study using a mixed-method design (Morse, 2003).

Ontology and Epistemology

The second angle on standpoint associated with research design is rooted in the assumptions in each design about how the research process works. These assumptions are related to ontology and epistemology.

Ontology

Ontology is the study of the nature of existence and being. It attempts to determine which entities might be considered to exist, separate from whether they are perceived or not, and thus could, in some sense, be said to "be," and how these entities may change over time (Noonan, 2008). If something exists, it is considered real and "true." Ontological beliefs are expressed in science through the assumptions on which research designs are based. In general, quantitative designs incorporate the assumption that some entities exist and can be accessed directly. The focus of researchers who use quantitative designs is on categorizing these entities and understanding relationships among them. This view is sometimes labeled as a "realist" perspective. In general, qualitative designs are more aligned with the idea that access to reality is mediated by factors such as language, culture, and gender and that because one cannot step outside these influences, one cannot access reality directly. This view is sometimes labeled as a "relativist" perspective.

Epistemology

Epistemology is the study of knowledge and, more precisely, how one can know what exists (Stone, 2008). Quantitative designs and early qualitative approaches are most closely aligned with the idea that anyone who follows a tightly prescribed approach may access the same information about fundamental entities. Kvale (1996) has used a mining metaphor to describe this approach to knowledge formation. Here data are considered to be nuggets of truth lying buried in the research participants. The interviewer's job is to uncover these nuggets and shape them into something useful. This position is sometimes called "objectivist." Later qualitative designs are more aligned with the idea that the researcher and the participant construct data, a position sometimes called "constructivist" or "postmodern." Kvale (1996) has used the traveler metaphor to describe this approach. A unique feature of the traveler metaphor is that in addition to the new knowledge that is created, both the researcher and the research participant might change. In this sense, research may be considered transformative.

Ontology, Epistemology, and Design

All research designs make assumptions about ontology and epistemology, although these assumptions might not be stated explicitly. Understanding these assumptions is important, because the assumptions shape the researcher's understanding of what data are. For example, if the researcher decides to use a design with a realist ontology and an objectivist epistemology, he or she would be more likely to view data as something to be "gathered," like picking flowers. However, if the researcher were to choose a design with a relativist ontology and constructivist epistemology, he or she would be more likely to view data as something to be "created" with the participant.

Research designs do not fall neatly along a continuum anchored at one end by a realist ontology and a positivist epistemology and at the other by a relativist ontology and a constructivist epistemology. Nevertheless, quantitative designs are generally realist and positivist in nature, whereas qualitative designs tend to have a more relativist ontology and constructivist epistemology.

Note that research designs are developed within a historical context and that they evolve over time. For example, early qualitative designs, such as traditional grounded theory (Glaser & Strauss, 1967), are considered to be closer to quantitative designs in their epistemology than are more recent approaches to grounded theory, such as those developed by Charmaz (2006) or Clarke (2005).

Reflexivity

Reflexivity is an analytic tool that can be used by qualitative researchers to make assumptions about standpoint, ontology, and epistemology more apparent. Reflexivity has many definitions, but it is essentially a strategy that focuses on the intersection between who the researcher is as a person and how he or she represents data (Pillow, 2003). Reflexivity is frequently confused with reflection. Chiseri-Strater (1996) distinguished between reflection and reflexivity by noting that, whereas reflection does not require an "other," reflexivity "demands both an other and some self-conscious awareness of the process of self-scrutiny" (p. 130).

Reflexivity is an important part of the analytic process, because it helps the researcher consider important questions such as "Who am I in relation to this study?" "What right do I have to study this research question?" and "To whom do the data belong?" As a result, reflexivity may be viewed as part of the process for establishing the credibility of a study and the validity of its findings (Dowling, 2006). The ideas that surface as a result of reflexivity show that the researcher is monitoring his or her standpoint as the study progresses.

Reflexivity also provides an opportunity for the researcher to examine how a study has influenced him or her. In recent paper, Ochieng (2010) provided a reflexive account of changes she experienced as a woman of African descent while conducting a study of families of African descent. Throughout her study she found herself taking the "side" of women who were experiencing conflicts with their husbands. She was surprised by this, noting that her study changed how she saw herself.

Given the importance ascribed to reflexivity, we generally assume that researchers choose carefully the words they use to report their study so that they accurately reflect the ontological and epistemological assumptions that were included in their study. Nevertheless, it is not uncommon to find that some qualitative researchers who used a constructivist epistemological perspective in their work, for example, included in the report of their findings a section called "data collection," a label that seems more appropriate to an objectivist epistemological perspective.

Whether one views data as "gathered" or "created" influences how one understands what data are. The gatherer of data views data as facts—as pieces of truth—and would expect individuals who were all part of some similar experience to tell similar stories. The creator of data, however, views data as representations of facts and would not be surprised if the stories told by individuals who all shared some experience were different, since each person's representation would be colored by his or her past experiences.

Qualitative researchers use many strategies to foster reflexivity. These strategies can range from activities such as discussions within their research teams and the maintenance of a research diary to nontextual approaches such as painting and photography. Many years ago I had an amazing student, Bruce Bailey, who taught me about reflexivity long before others were writing about it. Bruce was an ordained minister who decided to learn how to do qualitative research because he thought it would provide him with some additional insights into pastoral care aspects of his work. Given the age of his congregation, Bruce ministered to a number of people who had undergone a coronary artery bypass graft. He wanted to understand their experience and his responsibility to them as their pastor.

His approach to reflexivity was to write poetry while analyzing his data. One time I asked him if the ideas in the poem were his or were from the accounts told by the participants in his study, and his answer was simple. He laughed a big belly laugh and said, "Both!" He could easily track back both in the personal journal he kept about his experiences as a researcher and in the transcripts from his interviews to show me the roots of the ideas in his poetry. This is the essence of reflexivity.

Bruce's study focused on hope among female spouses of individuals who had undergone a coronary artery bypass surgery and were now in rehabilitation. He included a number of his poems in his dissertation. I am including one here that came at the end of a chapter on the attributes of hope to show the benefits of developing strategies that promote reflexivity and to honor Bruce's amazing insights into both his data and himself. In this poem, he said, he wanted to show the possibilities available through hope. Bruce died tragically in 2001, but I obtained permission from his wife, Pat, and children, Timothy Joel and Arynn Joy, to reprint his poem "Stolen Time," and the poem is presented in loving memory of him.

Stolen Time
It is intensely busy in the market place.
Demands real and expectations imagined
Stoop the shoulders,
Burden the mind,
Clog the arteries.
The seduced,
some of a necessity
known only to them,
others because of innocence lost,
are cut off from life's healing touch.

But, she is not there.
Absent, in spite of incessant gossip,
She is clothed in sloppy shirt and baggy jeans,
sitting amidst the uncut grass and weeds.
She sits with her beloved.
There, before the fire in its place
he reads, she knits.
They nibble on beef-steak tomato sandwiches;
pepper, no salt, for they are now heart healthy.

At dusk the wind and the waves harmonize in a love song.
She and her beloved answer the summons.
They walk to the top of the hill to watch
the deer and fox play in the field,
to stand under heaven's celestial lights.
There they wait until sunset's glow
and winds nurturing embrace
Cleanse every part of their pain.

She says: "Life is about basic things:
About nakedness and about innocence."
She searches his eyes, not for an answer,

But for awakening understanding.
He smiles.
She smiles.
They have come to themselves
in an instant of stolen time.
Her search ends another day in newness
for it has again led them back
to what is of vital importance.
The important thing is us!
The stars say so.
(Bailey, 1996)

Summary

Be sure to take the time to situate yourself in your study. Locate your standpoint. Think about who you are in relation to the study you want to conduct. How has your standpoint influenced your research question and the design of the study you are planning to conduct? The consequences of ignoring this phase of the research process are significant. If you do not understand your standpoint within research, it is easier for you to misunderstand what data are and to fail to "make sense" of those data. Find ways to develop your reflexive voice. Are you a poet? A painter? A photographer? A maker of notes? Create a plan for how you will track who you are in relation to your data as your study moves forward.

Exercises

1. Think about the study you are planning to do and write a paragraph outlining what you think the answer to the research question will be. Now write a second paragraph about the background for your "answer." Where did your answer come from? What do you know from your own work, reading, or personal experience that shaped your answer? Who has been influential in your thinking about this topic?

2. Write a paragraph about the general ideas about your research question from the standpoint of your discipline. Now pick one or two other disciplines and write another paragraph about the general ideas about your research question from these perspectives. For example, if I were to do this exercise, I would write about how some topic is generally viewed in

the nursing literature and then could write a paragraph about how this same topic is generally viewed in the health psychology and medical literature.

3. Think about your research topic. Do you want to tell the "insider" story or the "outsider" story? Why? What difference will this decision make it terms of who your participants are?

4. Review the methods section of two or three papers in an academic journal. How is the methods section labeled? See if you can get some clues about the assumptions regarding the ontological and epistemological perspective of the author(s).

5. Think about who you are in relation to the study you want to do. What approaches could you use to maintain ongoing internal dialogue about the interactions between you as the researcher and the stories of your participants? Try out a couple of approaches to see what works for you. Don't forget about nontext approaches such as painting and photography.

2. Talking about Experience

Each data-collection strategy used in qualitative research requires different information from study participants. When data are obtained using interviews, regardless of whether the interview is with an individual or a group, the primary task of the interviewer is to engage each participant in a particular type of conversation, one in which he or she describes experiences relevant to the research question (Kvale, 1996). Thus, the ensuing exchange is different from a conversation that may take place between two friends. The research interview takes place for a specific purpose developed by the researcher. Although the degree of control exerted over the interview by the researcher can vary, the research interview is one that may be differentiated from other kinds of conversations by the control the interviewer exerts over the exchange process. Despite this power gradient, however, both the interviewer and the study participant influence the quality of the information obtained.

In this chapter I discuss this point in more detail by focusing on demographic factors related to the interviewer and the participant that might influence data quality. I also explore the importance of preparing interviewers for the work of interviewing, factors to consider when deciding whom to interview, and special considerations related to interviews with individuals from vulnerable populations.

Demographic Factors Related to Data Quality

In a study recently completed by our research group (Porr, Olson, & Hegadoren, 2010), we wanted to interview individuals who had been diagnosed with a major depressive disorder. Participants were initially recruited through posters inviting interested individuals to call me. Partway through the study, however, we realized that although men commonly experience depression, no men had indicated an interest in our study. A clever young male graduate student suggested that we change the poster so that interested individuals would be invited to call him, and soon after we received numerous expressions of interest in our study from men diagnosed with depression. The opportunity to recruit depressed men following the change in our recruitment poster is an example of the influence of gender on the interview process. In our study, depressed men preferred to speak to a male interviewer.

A growing body of literature, now stretching back over several decades, documents the influence of various factors such as gender, race, ethnicity, sexual orientation, religion, political stance, and age on the quality of interview data (Warren, 2001). When a researcher is planning a study that will require the collection of data using interviews, he or she should remember that these considerations apply to both the interviewer and the study participants.

Part of an interviewer's personal identity comes from his or her disciplinary perspective. Each member of the research team brings a disciplinary perspective. Luff (1999) notes that one must always be aware of the interface between one's disciplinary preconceptions, which in her case were rooted in sociology, and the standpoints held by study participants.

Preparation of Interviewers for Interviewing

Interviewing is a complex task that requires careful preparation. Research teams must provide all interviewers with the knowledge and skills they require to gather the best possible interview data. Such training should include opportunities to conduct "practice" interviews and to engage in role-plays in which the interviewer has an opportunity to experience both the role of the interviewer and that of the study participant.

The training of interviewers is particularly important when the interview data will be collected in the context of a focus group. As focus groups generally include two members of the research team, one in the role of the moderator and one as a recorder of group interaction, trainees should be given an opportunity to practice both roles.

If an interviewer is new to qualitative research or the research team, the team may wish to consider providing several opportunities for the interviewer to observe interviews conducted by a more experienced member of the team before the new interviewer conducts an interview independently. The principal investigator is strongly encouraged to review the transcripts of the first few interviews conducted by new interviewers to ensure that the interviewer understands the interview process.

Deciding Whom to Interview

The decision about whom to interview is critical to the validity of a qualitative study, because it influences the adequacy of the sample (Morse et al., 2002). Spradley (1979) notes that the ideal participant is "thoroughly enculturated," currently involved in the topic of investigation, nonanalytic, and available. He also notes that the ideal interviewer is one who is unfamiliar with the topic and setting and thus less likely to overlook important details. This does not mean that researchers cannot conduct a study of a topic about which they are familiar; it means only that it is more difficult, because the researcher may inadvertently miss key ideas in the data. It is also the case, however, that being an insider might be beneficial, because a person who is an insider may have access to data that would not be available to others. This point became clear to me in my work on breast self-examination among Canadian women (Olson & Morse, 1996). In that case I met the inclusion criteria for my own study. I was studying women like me. In addition, the topic was one that was not easily discussed in social situations. It wasn't that discussions of breasts were somehow secret, but social conventions still limited the kinds of things one "could" say about touching one's own breasts. Over the course of that study, it seemed to me that my similarity to the participants provided a bridge of sorts across the social conventions constraining conversations about touching one's breast, and thus participants seemed more willing to discuss their experiences than if my demographic characteristics were different from theirs. Our interviews became conversations between two people who had both experienced these social conventions.

The researcher is more likely to recruit experienced, articulate study participants if he or she has taken the time to carefully focus the topic of the study. This may seem simple on the surface, but topics of interest to researchers often have many dimensions. For example, suppose that one wanted to study the process of becoming a mother. One could begin by recruiting women who were pregnant for the first time, but what about women who became mothers through adoption? What about women who did not formally adopt children but were viewed by children as the woman who raised them? What about women who cared for children through formal fostering programs? What about women who became pregnant but who had abortions or miscarriages? Are all of these women mothers?

A qualitative researcher may choose to limit an initial study to only some of the dimensions of a larger topic of interest but could, over time, conduct studies along all of the dimensions. For example, a researcher could begin a program of research by interviewing women who have given birth to their first child in the past year but might eventually conduct studies with all the groups mentioned above and then compare the findings across groups. The researcher could then extend this work further by undertaking this set of studies with women from different ethnic backgrounds and in different countries. In so doing, he or she could gradually build up a comprehensive, robust description of the meaning of being a mother.

Thinking about the dimensions of a topic helps the researcher to have a clearer notion about who would likely have experience that was relevant to the topic and would therefore be a good participant. This kind of thinking helps the researcher begin to define the population from within which participants will eventually be recruited.

Locating Experienced, Articulate Participants

The next step in deciding whom to interview is to find individuals who have had firsthand experience related to the research question and are able to describe their experience clearly. In general, if articulate individuals with extensive experience can be identified and recruited, fewer participants will be required.

One of the most important principles to remember relative to experience is that the acquisition of experience takes time. Qualitative researchers must ask themselves a key question about time as they plan their studies: how much time is required for a person to acquire "enough" experience to provide data of good quality? In planning the study of breast self-examination (Olson & Morse, 1996), I had the idea from my clinical experience in public health that there was certain knowledge about the body that was known and shared by Canadian women and that this knowledge influenced decisions about whether to do breast self-examination. In the process of determining whom to include in my study, I had to make a decision about how old a woman would have to be to have acquired the knowledge about breast self-examination that I wanted to study.

Canadians are generally considered adults when they are 18 years old, but I thought that it might take some years beyond that point for women to acquire the knowledge I wanted to tap. I was particularly interested in how body image and societal beliefs about breasts might influence breast self-examination practices. After extensive reading, I decided that I would recruit women who were at least 30 years old. By then, I argued, women likely would have had sufficient time as adult women to acquire the three things that were necessary for my study: experience with socially constructed ideas about breasts; experience within the health care system related to breasts and breast self-examination; and the language to describe these experiences.

Understanding Limits on the Ability to Talk about Experience

Sometimes an interview may begin well, but the participant has difficulty providing a detailed description of his or her experience, and as a result, the interview is quite short and "thin." This problem might come about because the participant's experience either is old or is limited in some way. The ideal participant is one whose firsthand experience is current and extensive, but such individuals, admittedly, can be hard to find. There is clearly some tension between these two attributes, since a person who is currently experiencing something may not have enough experience to describe it sufficiently.

Furthermore, an individual might have the experience required for a study but have difficulty describing it without becoming analytical and reflective, particularly if it occurred in the past. In that case, the reviewer should remind the participant to describe the details of the experience rather than what it meant to him or her.

Each researcher will have to sort out the time-experience issue in a manner best suited to the research question. Many approaches are possible. For example, in her study of how Iranian immigrants to Canada learn to use the Canadian health care system, Dastjerdi (2007) began by recruited individuals who had immigrated to Canada several years earlier. She asked these participants to describe their experiences using the Canadian health care system over time. Recruitment continued until she had sufficient data to construct an initial conceptual framework showing key aspects of the process used by her participants to become capable users of the Canadian health care system. She then recruited additional Iranian participants who were more recent immigrants to Canada. She used the descriptions provided by these later participants to test out some of theoretical ideas she had developed and to refine her framework as necessary.

Nuanced Experience

Sometimes the topic of interest is nuanced and is hard to distinguish from the context in which it occurs. All experience occurs in a context, but if the experience of interest cannot be distinguished from the context, it can be difficult to study. When a qualitative researcher is planning a recruitment strategy for a highly nuanced topic, one of his or her primary tasks is to design a recruitment plan that sharpens the boundaries around the topic of interest without compromising the ability to collect information about the context in which the data exist.

My work on fatigue provides an opportunity to discuss recruitment in a highly nuanced experience in more detail. Fatigue is a distressing symptom that is commonly experienced by individuals receiving treatment for cancer. Its appearance in the cancer symptom management literature is relatively recent, dating from the late 1970s, but fatigue has been discussed in other contexts such as occupational health since the 1930s. The etiology of fatigue, regardless of the context, has not been established, however. Moreover, the study of fatigue is complicated by the context in which it occurs. Among individuals with cancer, fatigue is generally considered to be a function of disease and treatment processes and comorbid conditions as well as other aspects of daily life.

To sharpen the boundaries of fatigue without removing it from its context, I compared fatigue experienced by individuals who were diagnosed with cancer to that experienced by individuals who had fatigue for other reasons. The first step was to review literature about fatigue in populations, other than those with cancer, in which fatigue was commonly reported. To tease out conceptual issues related to illness, I deliberately chose two populations in which fatigue was a central diagnostic feature of an illness (major depressive disorder and chronic fatigue syndrome) and two populations in which fatigue was commonly reported but was not related to illness (recreational runners and shift workers) (Olson & Morse, 2005).

In the second phase of the project, a qualitative study was conducted with individuals from each study population (Olson, 2007). This approach helped me to identify characteristics of fatigue that were common in all five study populations and to find descriptions of fatigue that distinguished it from other symptoms experienced by individuals with cancer. It also provided a way to show how the context shapes the ways in which fatigue is manifested.

Interviewing Individuals from Vulnerable Populations

The primary objective in any interview is to gather information that will help the research team answer the research question. Sometimes the ideal study participant is from a population that is considered "vulnerable" for some reason and in this circumstance requires additional considerations on the part of the researcher.

Vulnerability is a relatively new concept in social science research (Delor & Hubert, 2000). Chambers (1983) described vulnerability as having three dimensions: the risk of being exposed to crises; the risk of not having the resources to manage the crises; and the risk of being exposed to serious consequences by virtue of the crises. Vulnerability implies an increased susceptibility to harm or hurt. The interface between this increased susceptibility and the ability of an individual to provide an account of their experience is complex, and the related ethical issues are discussed in Chapter 5. The focus here is on issues related to the recruitment of individuals from vulnerable populations.

The examples in this section have been drawn from the literature on interviewing three of many vulnerable populations: children, older adults, and ill individuals. The primary task of the researcher is to think carefully about how an individual's vulnerability influences his or her ability to talk about experiences. Often it is the very fact of the individual's vulnerability that is of interest to the researcher, but this point must never take precedence over the potential harm, real or imagined, that could come to the participant as a result of participating in a study. The examples included below were selected to sensitize the reader to this important dimension of qualitative research and to provide a starting point for further discussion rather than to be a comprehensive discussion on this topic.

Interviewing Children

Setting the ethical issues associated with studying children aside, some researchers may wonder about the best way to obtain information about children. Should they interview them directly or ask parents about their children's ideas? Should they just watch the children? Eder and Fingerson (2001) note that although some authors advocate using only observational strategies to study children, they have successfully interviewed children as young as preschoolers. They add that such interviews provide an opportunity for children to speak in their own voice and to show how children construct descriptions about their experiences. By including children as participants in a study, the researcher gains access to information that is unfiltered by parents or other adults.

Children generally play and socialize in groups, and thus Eder and Fingerson (2001) encourage researchers to consider interviewing children in groups. These groups may be groups of other children or family groups. Such an approach naturalizes the research encounter for children and decreases the power differential between the researcher and the child. A challenge associated with interviewing very young children may be their limited language skills. Thus, Eder and Fingerson support using additional data-collection strategies such as observation.

Young children may be more comfortable if their parents are present, whereas older children might prefer to be interviewed without their parents. In their paper on young children with cystic fibrosis, MacDonald and Greggans (2008) noted that the presence of parents helped to keep the child focused on the interview and controlled disruptions. Parents provided a "scaffold" by adding comments to the child during the interview, such as, "Do you remember when… ?" Although such involvement by parents may be helpful, however, it clearly shapes the data that are obtained and thus may be problematic, particularly if the researchers are interested in views of children that are unprompted by others (Duncan et al., 2009).

Interviewing Older Adults

Some research questions require interviews with older adults. Such interviews present a different set of challenges than those with children (Wenger, 2001). First, the identification of participants requires the researcher to clearly define "older," a task that is more complex than it may appear on the surface. Who is old? Whom are they older than? Is this simply a matter of age?

Once these questions are answered, the interviewer must think about the best ways to manage issues such as sensory and cognitive impairment, should they exist. As individuals with hearing losses frequently supplement their understanding of conversations by lip reading, interviewers should position themselves so that the participant can clearly see the interviewer's face and should speak clearly.

Individuals whose vision is compromised may be reluctant to let the interviewer into their home, particularly if they live alone, because they have no way to verify the interviewer's identity. In this case, the interviewer may wish to seek the assistance of a friend or family member of the participant who would be willing to be present at the beginning of the interview and perhaps to stay with the participant for the duration of the interview, depending on the participant's preference. The main point here is that the researcher has an obligation to help the participant be as comfortable as possible with the interview process.

Although ideal participants are normally selected because they are articulate, one may choose to recruit an older adult because of his or her unique experience, despite difficulties in communicating these experiences. These difficulties may be associated with changes in the ability to speak following a stroke, with medications, or with cognitive impairment due to Alzheimer's disease or other forms of dementia. The interviewer who is patient and who can help the participant feel at ease will find that the quality of the data obtained under such circumstances is still excellent but that it may take longer to collect. It is particularly important to conduct interviews with individuals who have communication challenges in environments that are familiar and comfortable to them, such as their home. The material cues provided by familiar things such as photographs, furniture, dishes, and similar items may help the participant remember aspects of his or her experience that he or she would like to convey.

Interviewing Ill Individuals

Some interview questions require the collection of data from individuals who are ill. On occasion, the disease itself or its treatment might interfere with the ability of individuals to describe their experiences of illness (Morse, 2001). For example, their ability to speak may be compromised by conditions such as Parkinson's disease or a stroke. Other conditions such as schizophrenia are often characterized by altered verbal communication patterns that are difficult to interpret (Cretchley et al., 2010). In her interviews of individuals with schizophrenia, Lorencz (1991) found that conversations with participants also included their responses to other voices they heard. In yet other cases, when illness is associated with a traumatic event, the associated emotional shock may be such that the individual becomes withdrawn. Furthermore, some medications may interfere with a person's ability to think clearly. In such cases, the researcher must carefully consider whether to develop modifications to the interview process to facilitate data collection or whether to use some other forms of data collection, such as observation or document analysis to generate the data.

The nature of illness is such that it is often marked by acute and chronic phases that stretch over a period of time. Because interviews takes energy, an individual currently experiencing an acute phase of his or her illness may not have the energy required for an interview. If given the opportunity to participate in an interview later, however, once the acute phase has passed, the ill individual may welcome the opportunity to recount his or her experience (Morse, 2001).

Use of Shadowed Data

A lack of descriptive information, regardless of the reason, poses a serious problem for the qualitative researcher. Morse (2001) has suggested that one way to solve this problem is to use shadowed data. Shadowed data are essentially data obtained by interviewing someone who knows the participant well. In this case, the person being interviewed is asked to describe his or her observations of the experience of the person who is unable to tell his or her own story. For example, in our study of cancer patients we obtained shadowed data from the participants' family members and their nurses (Olson, Krawchuk, & Quddusi, 2007). If shadowed data are used, remember that observations of a person's experience could vary considerably from the description of the experience were the person able to provide the description him- or herself. Living an experience is different from observing it.

Summary

Interviews have the potential to generate data that are not accessible any other way. The interviewer and the study participant both have the potential to influence the quality of the interview data. The challenge of the researcher is to carefully weigh all the factors related to who the interviewer and the study participant are and to consider how to balance these factors to obtain the best possible data from the interviews.

Exercises

1. Think about your research question and then describe the characteristics of the ideal interviewer.
2. Choose a research topic and list five of its dimensions. Then write a research question that focuses on one of these dimensions. Make a list of whom you would interview to get firsthand experiential descriptions about each of these dimensions.
3. Think about your study topic. Are you an insider or an outsider? How comfortable will your participants be talking to you about the study topic? Are there ways you could increase their comfort with the interview process? Are you the ideal interviewer for your study, or do you need to ask another person to collect some of your data?

4. Make up a research question and then construct some possible interview questions. Work with a partner you don't know very well and set up the exercise so you have a chance to be both the interviewer and the participant. Write about how each role felt. What was it like to ask questions of a person who was essentially a stranger? How did it feel to describe your experiences to someone you didn't know very well?

5. Do you plan to interview young children, older adults, or ill individuals? What particular challenges do you anticipate, and how do you plan to manage them?

6. Think of a situation in relation to the study you are planning in which shadowed data may be helpful. Why did you decide to obtain shadowed data? Whom will you interview? What will you ask them to talk about? How might you determine any discrepancies between the shadowed data and data that would be provided by the participants if they were able to describe their own experience?

7. Construct a "shadowed data" experiment by writing down your experience of some event and then asking someone you know who was also present to write down their description of your experience. Compare the two descriptions. What kinds of similarities and differences do you notice?

3. Approaches to Data Generation

ardly a day passes that one does not encounter an interview in some form. For example, an interview could be part of a late-night television program or an article in a popular magazine. Most often interviews are not conducted for research purposes. Readers interested in the history of interviewing may enjoy a recent book on this topic by Fontana and Prokos (2007).

In this chapter I discuss the specific kinds of interviews that are conducted for research purposes and the way one goes about generating data in each of them. Structured interviews are most often found in quantitative studies such as surveys. Because this book is part of a series on qualitative research, this chapter focuses primarily on the kinds of interviews used in qualitative studies, but structured interviews are briefly discussed. I have outlined the strengths and weaknesses of each kind of interview and given examples of when each kind of interview might be used.

Interviews in the Context of Research

There are two basic kinds of interviews: formal and informal. Both kinds of interviews may be conducted with either individuals or groups. Each kind of interview is used under different circumstances. Table 3.1 provides a brief description of each type of interview, including its knowledge requirements, strengths, weaknesses, and uses.

Formal Interviews with Individuals

Formal interviews take place at a time jointly set aside for the interview and are generally recorded so that they can be transcribed to facilitate analysis. They are commonly used as the primary data-collection method in

Table 3.1
Kinds of Interviews

Kind of Interview	Knowledge Required	Strengths	Weaknesses	Uses
Formal Structured	Extensive	Standardized Easy to use Easy to summarize Data can be gathered quickly	Responses are limited to the questions included Limited control over the interview by the participant	Summarizing population characteristics or trends Gathering data for testing of hypotheses
Formal Unstructured	Minimal	Creates maximum space for the participant to tell his or her story. Maximum control over the interview by the participant	Discussion can be wide ranging, easy to lose focus	First interview
Formal Guided	Minimal	Planned questions give a common starting point for early interviews	Danger of inadvertently limiting descriptions	First interview
Formal Semistructured	Modest	Allows interviewer to follow up on ideas raised by participants	Participants not necessarily all asked the same questions More complicated to analyze	Later in a study to seek clarification Focus groups

Table 3.1
Continued

Kind of Interview	Knowledge Required	Strengths	Weaknesses	Uses
Formal Group	Minimal-Modest	Quick, able to observe interactions among group members	Possibly some reluctance to discuss experience in a group setting	Focus groups Families
Informal	Not applicable	Able to collect important data shared spontaneously outside the formal interview	No opportunity to record conversations	Unplanned interactions

both quantitative and qualitative research designs. They can be structured, unstructured, or semistructured.

Structured Interviews

Structured interviews are used when knowledge on a given topic is sufficiently large that its dimensions are known, and thus this type of interview is well suited for use in quantitative research designs. The existing knowledge base guides the development of questions that are specific and focused. Participants are given a limited range of response options. Given the underlying knowledge base, the responses to structured interviews can be linked theoretically and used to advance knowledge in the field under investigation.

Structured interviews are most often found in the context of survey research. For example, in a survey being conducted for community development purposes, a participant might be asked if he or she has lived in a certain neighborhood for five years or more and, if so, to rate his or her satisfaction with proximity to various amenities such as recreation/leisure facilities, grocery shopping, and restaurants on a scale of 1 to 5, with 5 being "very satisfied." The questions in a structured interview resemble those incorporated in a questionnaire, with the only real difference being that the questions in a structured interview are read to the participant by the interviewer, whereas in a questionnaire the participant answers the questions independently.

It is not uncommon for a short series of open-ended questions to be added to the end of a survey. For example, the questions in the paragraph above could be followed by a question such as "What is the best thing about living in your neighborhood?" or "How would you describe this neighborhood to someone who was thinking about moving here?"

Raising the possibility of including open-ended questions in a survey provides an opportunity to stop briefly to discuss an interesting methodological question: how would one describe the design of a survey that includes open-ended questions? Although qualitative data are obtained in such studies, it would be more appropriate to describe the design of such studies as "mixed." Mixed-method designs may be planned around the requirements for reliability and validity of either qualitative or quantitative designs, with various data collection strategies not normally found in the preferred design added as required by the research question (Morse, 2003). Thus, one may speak of a mixed-method design as having either a qualitative drive or a quantitative drive. A survey with added open-ended questions is a good example of a mixed-method design with a quantitative drive, since surveys are generally planned around the requirements of quantitative designs such as representative sampling. For a survey to be considered to have a qualitative drive, it would need to meet the requirements of qualitative designs, such as purpose sampling, prolonged engagement in the field, and data saturation (Morse et al., 2002), and this is seldom the case.

The main hallmark of structured interviews is that all participants are asked the same questions in the same order, and thus one of the strengths of this type of interview is that the results are easy to summarize. A second strength is that structured interviews generally take less time to complete than other kinds of interviews. A key limitation of structured interviews, however, is that they provide very limited opportunity for the participant to add new ideas that are not addressed by the survey questions but are central to his or her experience. Thus, structured interviews may constrain the ways in which a participant would otherwise describe an experience.

Interviews for the Early Phases of Qualitative Studies

When sufficient knowledge is not available to guide the development of interview questions, a different approach to interviewing is required. In this case, the researcher must find a way to begin sketching out the dimensions of the information that will eventually be used to answer the research question. Two kinds of interviews are particularly helpful in this regard, unstructured interviews and guided interviews. Excerpts from hypothetical interviews using both of these formats are included in the Appendix.

Unstructured Interviews

The objective of an unstructured interview is to begin a relationship with the study participant and create a space within which the participant feels free to tell his or her story. The participant thus has maximum control over the interview process (Corbin & Morse, 2003). As shown in the unstructured interview included in the Appendix, the interviewer using this format does not have any "questions" that are "asked" per se, but requests information by introducing some very broad topics for discussion within the context of a general conversation. For example, if the research question were focused on the experience of becoming a parent, the researcher might begin the interview by saying "Please describe something that has happened to you that would help me understand what becoming a parent has been like for you." At some point in the conversation, the participant locates an anchor to which he or she can "tie" his or her story, and description of experience begins. A topic that works well with one participant may not be helpful at all with the next participant, however. As a result, comparison across stories is tedious and time consuming.

Because unstructured interviews are commonly used for the first interview with a study participant, they are wide ranging, and some content may appear to wander "off topic." The interviewer's task is to determine which elements of the interview are relevant to the study and how they are related. At a loss to know whether the participant has indeed wandered "off topic" or I am simply not seeing relationships that are apparent to him or her, I have sometimes simply asked a participant to help me locate the connections between ideas by saying, "You started by taking about xxx and now you are talking about yyy. It would be helpful for me to know whether these two things are connected for you and, if so, how they are connected."

Guided Interviews

The "guided" interview is another approach commonly used for the first interview with a study participant. The term *guided* here is used to indicate that the interviewer has constructed some opening questions, and, as shown in the excerpt included in the Appendix, the interview is therefore slightly more constrained than an unstructured interview. Using this approach, the researcher prepares a set of three or four general, broad questions designed to help the participants find a way to begin telling their stories. Continuing with the example from above in which the research question was about the experience of becoming a parent, an example of a question for a guided interview could be "How is your life different now compared to how it was before your baby was born?"

There is some advantage, particularly for the beginning researcher, to having a common set of questions to use as a starting point for an interview. The danger, however, is that in the process of constructing the questions, the researcher may inadvertently exclude an important aspect of the experience that a participant would otherwise have described.

Semistructured Interviews for the Later Phases of Qualitative Studies

In semistructured interviews, researchers use information they have acquired to construct questions that are more focused. A semistructured interview is commonly used later in a research study, when the researcher is seeking further clarification about some area that was discussed in earlier interviews and is relevant to the research question. An excerpt of a hypothetical semistructured interview is included in the Appendix. Because this approach may be used to follow up on information a participant has provided in an earlier interview, participants are not necessarily all asked the same questions. In the course of beginning to saturate data categories, however, the researcher may decide to use a question that was particularly helpful in an interview late in the study when they conduct follow-up interviews with participants interviewed earlier. For example, the interviewer might say, "Since I talked to you last time, other participants have mentioned xxx. If xxx has also been part of your experience, please describe a time when this took place."

Formal Interviews with Groups

There are occasions in some qualitative studies when the researcher may find it helpful to interview a group of individuals. Group interviews are difficult to manage because participants are encouraged to respond to questions posed by the researcher as well as comments and questions posed by other members of the group. Thus, the data are complex, and the recording of such data requires careful documentation of both the participants' responses and their interactions.

Focus Groups

The most common form of the group interview is the focus group. Focus groups have historically been used in fields such as marketing to acquire feedback on various topics or to test-market new products, but they are being used increasingly in qualitative research. Focus groups are conducted when the researcher is interested in the interactions that occur among group members as well as their responses to questions posed by the interviewer. The use of focus groups simply to collect data quickly or to collect data that would be more appropriately collected using individual interviews is discouraged.

The semistructured interview format is commonly used for focus groups. An excerpt of a hypothetical focus group interview using semistructured questions is included in the Appendix. The moderator generally plans a set of four or five questions and tries to ensure that all are discussed over the course of the focus group. The content for the questions is drawn from existing literature, including theoretical material, or information obtained through some other means earlier in the study. Studies often include several focus groups. Although the same questions are used in each focus group within a given study, they might not be asked in the same order each time.

Interview data obtained from groups are much more complex than those obtained from individuals, because focus-group data include responses both to the moderator's questions and to the questions and comments of other people in the group. As a result, the nature of the data is different from that of data obtained from individual interviews, and the two types of data cannot be used interchangeably.

When analyzing focus group data, in addition to the actual text from the interview, the researcher must also consider issues such as the social context of the group, nonverbal data, and the sequential nature of the interactions when developing the interpretation of the data (Carey, 1995; Hollander, 2004). Because of the complexity of the data, focus groups are often conducted by a moderator and an individual who records the social interaction. The moderator asks the interview questions while the recorder monitors nonverbal data and tracks participation of all members so that the moderator can help those who have not participated join the conversation if they wish.

In addition to their usual uses, focus groups can be helpful during the planning phase of a study to help work out topics and questions for individual interviews. For example, in our study of fatigue in individuals with lung and colorectal cancer (Olson et al., 2002), which was a mixed-methods study with a qualitative drive, we conducted several focus groups with patients who had completed their treatments to get input on the best ways to frame the topics we wanted to discuss.

There are many kinds of focus groups, and a complete discussion is beyond the scope of this book. Readers interested in learning more about focus groups and how to conduct them might wish to review the work of David Morgan (1997) or Richard Krueger (2009) on this topic.

Family Interviews

Group interviews may also be conducted in situations in which a group such as a family, rather than an individual, is the intended unit of analysis or in situations in which one was intending to interview an individual but a second person was present and contributed to the interview. The use

42

of group interviews in this context is controversial. Although one could argue that family members should be interviewed separately so that they feel less constrained by other family members, our experience is that such an approach has the potential for generating conflict within some families. Members of our team found, for example, that family members sometimes asked the interviewer what other family members had said. We reminded the family members that we could not disclose this information, given issues of confidentiality as outlined in the consent, and encouraged them to discuss their concerns with their family member. Nevertheless, we were concerned that our decision to conduct interviews of family members separately had inadvertently triggered conflict within the family, or at least a concern that "family secrets" may be shared inappropriately.

Researchers planning to interview family groups must be clear about their reasons for interviewing the family together or separately. If the researcher's interest is in the family's perspective, he or she must determine how to get the family story, not just the story of each individual family member.

Morris (2001) outlined some issues related to group interviews, based on her work with individuals who had cancer and their family caregivers. When given a choice of individual or group interviews, she found that her study participants frequently requested to be interviewed together. She noted that although the group interview shared some characteristics with a standard focus group in that participants were encouraged to respond to the questions posed by the researcher and to comments and questions posed by other group members, there was an added level of intimacy, given the relationships of the group members to one another. Although families with problematic dynamics would not likely volunteer to participate in a study, one could imagine other situations in which it might be more useful to interview family members separately.

There are some benefits to including both individual and group interviews when studying dyads (Eisikovits and Koren, 2010). By comparing themes across interviews with each participant individually to themes that arise when both individuals in a dyad are interviewed together, the researcher is able to explore views held in common and views held separately, as well as views apparent to one partner but not apparent to the other.

An important difference between family interviews and focus group interviews is related to representativeness. In the group interview with a family, all members of a family could be included, and thus the data obtained could be considered to represent the views of the whole family. Participants in a focus group, in contrast, are drawn from some large population. Depending on how the focus group members were selected, the data obtained might not be representative of the population from which they were drawn.

Informal Interviews

Informal interviews do not take place at a specific time set aside for the interview. Rather, they occur as part of normal, everyday conversations when the researcher happens to be interacting with individuals within the research environment, as is often the case in studies that use an ethnographic or participatory action design. Thus, one does not have any interview questions per se, and it is difficult to record such interviews. As a result, after the interview is over, the researcher must prepare a field note in which the material discussed in the interview is described in as much detail as possible.

Informal interviews raise an important ethical issue. Although the researcher may have obtained consent from the person with whom he or she is conversing, the person might not realize that the researcher is "collecting" data. Recheck participants' willingness to participate in the study each time data are collected, regardless of whether the context is formal or informal.

Given the nature of informal interviews, sometimes an individual from whom consent has not yet been obtained provides information that is relevant to the research question. Should this happen, the researcher should obtain consent to include the information before formally incorporating the data. In this situation, it is not uncommon to request consent following the interview. It is also possible that sometime after a conversation, perhaps several days, the researcher may realize that he or she learned some important information in an earlier conversation with someone from whom they do not yet have consent. Again, the researcher must obtain consent to include this information before formally incorporating the data.

Generating Data in Early Interviews

Figuring out how to begin an interview is difficult. The way an interview is started must account for whether the researcher is interviewing an individual or a group, the kind of interview, the research questions, and the context that surrounds the research questions. If the opening is not sufficiently broad, the researcher will not have sufficient contextual information to interpret the data. If the opening is too broad, however, the researcher runs the risk of gathering irrelevant information.

When beginning the early interviews, the researcher should remember that although he or she may have developed some "guiding" questions, the objective is not to "guide" an interview. Indeed, the interviewer should avoid all subtle indications that this is intended, since this would be a major threat to the validity of the data. Rather, one wishes to open a conversation with the participant. The key message should be "I am interested in your story and whatever you want to tell me about it." When conducting an unstructured group interview, the researcher should make a few introductory statements before beginning to outline the parameters of the group process—for example, "I would like to know your thoughts about xxx. Please feel free to also comment on points raised by others in the group."

Some years ago, a member of a research team on which I worked obtained the consent from a study participant and then simply said "Any time you're ready." I was amazed by the incredibly rich data he obtained using that simple introduction but should add that although I have tried a similar approach, I have not been as successful. Nevertheless, I think he had a good understanding of what was required in the first interview. The primary characteristic of the opening approach used at the beginning of a study must be broad and open ended.

It is not uncommon for individuals who have not been interviewed in the context of a qualitative study in the past to feel uncertain about how to begin. Keep in mind that although the participant has signed the consent form and thus has some idea about the purpose of the study, the idea that he or she is simply being asked to describe an experience may initially feel awkward to them. Every qualitative researcher will develop strategies that work best for him or her, but one approach is to begin with a very general statement. I have used statements such as "As I mentioned in the letter attached to the consent form for this study, I am interested in learning more about how things have been going for you lately." The idea here is to let the participant know that the researcher is interested in the participant's story as a whole. Prompts can be used later to focus the interview, if necessary. For example, in my work on fatigue, I listened for words and phrases related to fatigue and asked participants to tell me more in those areas.

One may need to experiment with various ways to begin an interview. The goal is to help participants move past any introductory questions asked

45

and settle into "telling" their story rather than "answering" the researcher's questions. Beginning researchers often make the mistake of wanting to rush directly to their topic of interest and use their research questions as initial opening questions. The beginning of the interview needs to provide context for interpretation of the data. The opening comments by the research should invite description ("Tell me about...," "Please give an example...," "Please tell me about a time when...") rather than analysis ("How did you feel about... ?"). The "asking" for information needs to be gentle and open. This descriptive approach helps participants understand their role as a describer of their experience. By using questions that are analytic in nature, the researcher runs the risk of turning the research interview into a therapeutic exchange and thus of inadvertently moving beyond the limits of the consent.

Most research ethics committees require that the researcher submit several possible topics or questions that will be used to being the interviews. Funding review panel members also expect the researcher to provide a list of possible topics or questions for early interviews, because this lets the reviewers know that the researcher has thought about some possible strategies for beginning the interviews he or she is planning to conduct.

As the initial interview progresses, the participant (or participants, in the case of a group interview) will pause more, and the pace of the interview will slow down. The interviewer must learn to resist the urge to interject or ask more questions immediately and to wait until the participant indicates that he or she is finished with his or her comments or simply stops talking. At the end of the participant's story, there is time for the interviewer to ask the participant to elaborate on the points about which more information is needed—for example, "You mentioned xxx. Please tell me more about that."

Generating Data in Follow-Up Interviews

Prolonged engagement in the field is one of the hallmarks of qualitative research and is critical to the rigor of a qualitative study (Morse et al., 2002). By spending time in the field and really getting to know the participants, the researcher is more likely to get beyond the initial superficial responses to any questions he or she may ask and to obtain the information required to answer the research question. For this reason, qualitative research is a time-intensive endeavor. In most research designs, participants are interviewed at least twice, but in ethnographic studies, oral histories, or studies using participatory action designs, one might interview participants many times.

There are several ways to begin a follow-up interview, but a simply strategy is to say, "I have a couple of things I'd like to follow up on. But before we do that, is anything else you've thought of since we last talked that you would like to add?" Once the participant has finished with any additional comments, the researcher could continue by saying, "When we spoke last, you mentioned xxx. Please tell me more about that."

Subsequent interviews also provide an opportunity to return to participants interviewed early in a study with new information that surfaces in interviews with individuals recruited later in a study. Remember to mention this possibility in the consent form and to remind participants of this possibility, including their right to refuse such interviews even though they initially gave consent. The opportunity to move back and forth among the study participants in this manner increases opportunities to saturate data categories, and thus one is likely to require fewer participants.

At the end of the interview the interviewer should always ask the participant if there is anything else that he or she thinks is relevant to the topic of the study that has not been discussed ("Is there anything else that would be helpful for me to know that we haven't discussed?"). This is often the point at which some of the most important data in a study surface. Participants have a wealth of information that they are generally willing to share, but they might not do so, because they do not recognize its value. This information may stretch far beyond the interviewer's thoughts about the topic. To access this information, interviewers must convey that they are open to hearing it, even though they might not have asked explicitly about it.

Data Generation and Design

Never lose track of the research questions that drive a study. This is because the research questions, in turn, drive the choice about the best design for the study, and the design selected has implications for how the interview questions are framed and for the interviewing process. Although interviewing is a common data-collection strategy across most, if not all, qualitative designs, the nature of the interview questions is different.

In studies based on a grounded-theory design, for example, interview questions are focused on social or social-psychological processes. The goal in grounded theory is to identify a central problem and to situate it within a basic social process. The researcher uses grounded theory because his or her primary interest is in learning more about how meaning arises as a function of social interaction. The interviewer begins with an unstructured interview approach and uses broad, open-ended questions to learn about the participant's experience. As the study progresses and the relationships among main ideas from the early interviews become clearer, the interview approach becomes semistructured, and the interview questions become more focused. This shift is essential in more fully elaborating the relationships among the main ideas, thus making it possible for the researcher to formulate a theory about these relationships (Glaser, 1978).

In studies using an ethnographic design, however, the purpose of the study is to learn about culture. *Culture* is a word that has so many meanings that researchers are sometimes reluctant to use it. Here I have deliberately chosen the definition provided by Spradley (1979), who said that culture refers "to the acquired knowledge that people use to interpret experience and generate social behavior" (p. 5). Beginning with an unstructured interview format, the focus of early ethnographic interviews is on trying to make beliefs and values explicit. This important difference can be seen more clearly in studies that use an institutional ethnographic approach, where the objective is to uncover how societal institutions shape experience (Smith, 1996). For example, using an institutional ethnographic approach, Sinding (2010) used interviews, along with other data sources, to show how disparities are produced in the routine provision of cancer care.

An additional point related to the intersection between design and interviewing is that in some designs, such as grounded theory, interviews may be the primary data source, whereas in other designs, such as ethnography and photovoice, interviews might be one of several data sources used. For example, Drew, Duncan, and Sawyer (2010) asked young people with asthma, diabetes, or cystic fibrosis to photograph aspects of their daily life and then interviewed them about the photographs they created. Generating data from several sources generally produces results that are richer and more substantial, but this benefit must be balanced against the additional expense and time required to generate, analyze, and integrate findings.

Summary

The nature of the interview conducted in the context of a qualitative study is distinctly different from interviews that take place in other, nonresearch settings. Interviews may be formal or informal, and may be conducted with individuals or groups. Although the choices related to which kind of interview to use may vary with the design and the phase of the study in which the researcher is working, each has the potential to yield rich data that cannot be accessed any other way. The decisions about the type of interview to conduct must be made deliberately and for reasons that fit with the purpose of the study.

Throughout the interview, the interviewer must say just enough that the participant feels relaxed, comfortable, and at ease. The invitations to conversation and the questions asked play a central role in maintaining the conversational space. The use of questions early in the study that are too focused might limit the ability of participants to share their whole experience, and the continued use of broad questions late in the study might prevent researchers from refining their results and answering their research questions.

Exercises

1. Think about your research topic. What kind of interviews do you plan to use? Formal? Informal? Why?
2. Imagine that you are preparing to interview an individual for the first time, and develop one or two possible ways to open the interview using an unstructured interview format. How will you explain to the participant what you want him or her to talk about? Now find a friend who is willing to role-play an interview with you. Try out your introductory comments. How did your comments work? Ask your friend for feedback about how to make them more "inviting." Switch roles and ask your friend to use another of the strategies you developed for opening an interview. Which approach worked better? How does it feel to be interviewed? How does it feel to be the interviewer?
3. Think about how the design of your study will influence what you will say to your participants. Try adjusting your research questions so that the research design would change and then compare the opening comments for a first interview from the standpoint of each design.
4. How many interviews do you think you would like to have with each of your study participants? Why?
5. Although it is hard to plan questions for follow-up interviews before you have completed your initial interviews, make a list of some of the topics you think might arise that would require follow-up.

6. Think about a situation in which you might prefer to conduct an interview with a group rather than an individual. Make a list comparing the strengths and limitations of individual and group interviews. Create a research question and then prepare two or three semistructured questions that you could use to begin the focus group discussion. Practice them with a few friends. Take turns being the moderator, the assistant, and the study participants. What are the similarities and differences in the role of the moderator of a focus group and the role of the interviewer of a single participant?

7. What are some strategies that could be used to keep track of participation in a focus group?

4. The Logistics of Interviewing

This chapter focuses on some logistical issues related to interviewing. I begin with a discussion about modes of interviewing and some of the factors that influence the choices about which modes to use. I also discuss some practical aspects of the interview process, including note taking during interviews, pacing the interview, managing interviews about sensitive topics, ending the interview and the interview relationship, and debriefing following an interview.

Modes of Interviewing

There is a growing body of literature about the relationship between interview mode and data. "Interview mode" refers to the manner in which the interview data are obtained. The challenge for the researcher is to choose the mode or modes that result in the best descriptions of the experience under investigation. The most common modes are the face-to-face interview and the phone interview, but with the growth of the Internet, a number of other options, such as e-mail and "chat," have become available.

There is a debate in the literature about the influence of interview mode on the data the researcher is able to obtain. In their study of correctional officers' and prisoners' perceptions about visiting county jail inmates, Sturges and Hanrahan (2004) reported that there were no differences in data obtained from face-to-face and phone interviews. McCoyd and Schwaber-Kerson (2006), however, used e-mail, face-to-face interviews, and phone interviews to obtain information from women who had terminated a pregnancy following diagnosis of fetal anomaly and reported that that although all three modes were successful in generating important information, the e-mail interview approach seemed to generate more "detailed and thoughtful responses" (p. 403). Bosio and colleagues argue that the findings of any qualitative study result from the intertwining of decisions related to design, which they label "theory of theory," and decisions about how data will be gathered, which they label "theory of technique" (Bosio, Graffigna, & Lozza, 2008; Graffigna, Bosio, & Olson, 2010). There are likely many factors that could influence similarities and differences in interview data obtained using different modes, and thus researchers are well advised to remember that the data collected using different modes might not be equivalent.

The decisions about which interview mode(s) to choose are complex. The researcher must balance data quality with the interactions among issues such as need for nonverbal and/or contextual data, the sensitivity of the topic, accessibility, cost, and researcher safety.

Need for Nonverbal Data

Each researcher needs to think carefully about the degree to which his or her research question requires analysis of both the verbal and the nonverbal data. For example, is it important to see the participants' facial expressions or their general appearance? Although interviews obtained using modes other than the face-to-face mode have many advantages, the researcher must remember that such approaches may alter the collection of nonverbal data. Interviews collected over the Internet or the phone prevent the researcher from seeing the face of the research participant firsthand, but the skilled phone interviewer might still be able to hear signs of distress, for example, in the voice of the participant, and users of the Internet are developing textual practices for conveying emotion. In their paper on the use of e-mail to collect data from women who terminated a pregnancy following a diagnosis of fetal anomaly, for example, McCoyd and Schwaber-Kerson (2006) noted that the participants used :: to indicate that they were crying. With the rapid expansion of Web-based communication, other similar conventions will likely develop. The important thing for the researcher to remember is that it is his or her task to describe experience. Whether one sees the tears firsthand or reads :: in the e-mail of a weeping participant, one has information about the nature of the experience for the participant, which can then be considered in light of the other data in the study.

Need for Contextual Data

In general, all qualitative designs require the researcher to interpret the data collected. Contextual data are central to the interpretation process.

Contextual data are routinely and easily collected when data are collected in person. While conducting a face-to-face focus group, for example, one often makes notes about the physical environment. In addition to facilitating interpretation, this information may be used to frame further lines of questioning. When interviews are not collected face-to-face, however, the researcher must think of other ways to obtain contextual data, realizing that his or her understanding of the context may be different than if the researcher had collected the data face-to-face.

Sensitivity of the Topic

If the sensitivity of the topic is related to a social taboo or behavior that is considered inappropriate, participants may prefer the anonymity afforded by a phone interview. In their study of alcohol consumption, for example, Greenfield, Midanik, and Rogers (2000), found that telephone interviews increased participants' perceptions of anonymity. If the sensitivity of the topics is related to its emotional nature, however, Sturges and Hanrahan (2004) note, participants may find it easier to discuss their experiences face to face.

Access to Participants

Several issues related to participant accessibility may influence the mode used for the interview. The most common accessibility issue is related to geographical location. A participant's geographical location may be such that the collection of a face-to-face interview is prohibited by cost or time. This is often the case in such studies as life histories. In this situation, the researcher must choose some other interview mode. Phone interviews are probably the most common alternative, but this limits participation to those who have a phone.

More recently some researchers have started to use options available through the Internet, such as e-mail and synchronous or asynchronous chat. In the study mentioned earlier in this chapter, McCoyd and Schwaber-Kerson (2006) compared e-mail interviews with those obtained by phone and face-to-face and found that e-mail interviews appeared to facilitate inclusion of participants who were isolated for various reasons and thus often overlooked or ignored and not included in other studies.

Use of the Internet to gather both individual and group interviews has meant that researchers are able to obtain information that was previously unavailable to them. Fleitas (1998) developed an Internet-based strategy to augment data obtained through interviews and focus groups about the experiences of children with chronic illnesses from around the world, and Meier and colleagues (2006) used an online chat format in a study designed to gather information about the best way to design a program for cancer survivors. The availability of chat and various other platforms for meetings over the Internet, particularly those with video capability, has also meant that focus groups are no longer limited to face-to-face interactions. The technical aspects of Internet-based meetings can be frustrating, however, particularly when the researcher is trying to manage issues related to fire-walls, so I strongly advised those planning Internet-based interviews to have team members who can help manage any technical issues.

Accessibility to participants might also be limited by the nature of the setting. For example, researchers working in industry may find that although a commercial enterprise has given permission for the employees to take part in a study, they may restrict access to their site because of the confidential nature of their work or safety issues related to manufacturing processes. In this case, the participants may agree to be interviewed face to face at some other location or may prefer to be interviewed by phone.

Accessibility might also be a function of participant burden. There may be some participants who would like to participate in a study but who find face-to-face interviews burdensome as a result of such issues as health status, time constraints, or family responsibilities. In this case face-to-face interviews may still be possible if the interviewer is able to travel to the home of the participant. In general, participants are comfortable in their homes, and thus the home provides a good interview environment. In some cases, however, it is difficult to minimize interruptions from other family members such as small children, so the quality of the interview is compromised. For these reasons, the researcher may opt to conduct a phone interview.

Despite the obvious advantages related to the use of the Internet, some challenges also exist. For example, the use of the Internet for the collection of interview data requires research teams with technological skills (Meier et al., 2006). Unique textual practices associated with online chat also raise questions about its suitability as the sole date source (Davis et al., 2006). Both phone-based interviews and Internet-based approaches to interviewing are limited to those who have access to phones, and computers, and high-speed Internet. This limitation is not insignificant, because it limits the population from whom the researcher may draw participants. The researcher choosing to rely primarily on phone- or Internet-based interviewing must ask him or herself, "Are there people I need to include in my study that I am systematically excluding because of the way I am collecting my data?"

Safety

Researchers in the social sciences sometimes find that their research has the potential to take them into environments in which their personal safety may be potentially threatened. There is surprisingly little written about this aspect of research. The nature of qualitative research, with its focus on experience, makes it particularly useful in understanding environments that are unsafe.

Interviewers are advised to pay attention to any cues or intuitive feelings that their safety might be compromised and to remove themselves from such situations as quickly as possible. In addition, the research team may wish to create an interview log for studies in which safety might be an issue. Interviewers could then note the date, time, and address of each interview before they leave the office, and then log the time when they return to the office. By monitoring the log, the principal investigator would be able to determine quickly whether a participant seems to be delayed at an interview and can follow up as needed. As an additional safety precaution, all interviewers should be instructed to carry a cell phone so they can call for help. In their paper on the management of fieldwork in dangerous settings, Belousov and colleagues (2007) describe the strategies they developed to protect research team members in unsafe environments. They noted that although they were able to collect data firsthand, there may be situations in which researchers need to collect their data using other strategies, such as phone interviews, because of safety concerns.

Practical Issues Associated with the Interview Process

Setting the Stage for the Interview

Kvale (1996) likened the interview to a kind of performance that takes place on a stage. It is useful, therefore, to think about how to set up the stage so that one is able to facilitate the best possible outcome. What are the core components that must be present for the performance to "work"?

Begin by thinking about the local customs. Are there practices that must be followed for participants to be comfortable talking about their experience in the interview setting? How might the setting influence the participant's comfort with the interview process?

Although the purpose of the interview is generally included in the materials that accompany the consent forms, make sure that the participant is clear about this purpose. For example, before beginning the interview, the researcher might find it helpful to remind the participant of the purpose. In my studies on fatigue in shift workers, for example, I began by saying:

> As we discussed, this study is about the experience of fatigue in people who do shift work. To set the stage, I would like you to begin by telling me about a few situations that would help me understand what being a shift worker is like.

Once the participant finished describing the situations he or she selected, I sometimes asked, "How is it different from working a days-only job?" The danger in any interview is to rush into the central domain of the research question too quickly. Unless one understands the context surrounding the research question, the analysis will be very thin and general.

Before the interview begins, find out if the participant has any questions. Although participants are always asked if they have questions at the time the consent is obtained, some questions can arise later, after participants have had more time to think about the study. Ensure that the participants understand that no matter when these questions arise, they may always ask them.

Note Taking during the Interview

Beginning researchers often wish to bring a notepad with them to the interview so that they can jot down ideas to which they wish to return. There are pros and cons associated with this practice, but in my experience this approach is often distracting to participants. I strongly encourage my students to develop the skill of taking mental notes instead and then using these notes as a foundation for their subsequent questioning. This is a skill that takes practice.

Pace of the Interview

Many factors come together to influence the pacing of an interview. If the interview requires special modifications owing to unique characteristics of the participants or setting, the interview may proceed more slowly. Ill individuals will have limited energy and may prefer to take breaks during the interview or to limit the length of the interview. Interviews conducted in the home setting sometimes proceed more slowly, especially if young children are present and interrupt the interview. The main point to remember is that the interviewer should be aware that he or she may need to alter the pace of the interview, depending on the needs of the participant.

Managing Interviews about Sensitive Topics

Sometimes an interview may seem to lack detail or be short in length because the material is difficult to discuss. Topics that are emotionally charged are particularly prone to this problem; acknowledge this possibility with participants and in the consent form. Some institutional review boards may require the researcher to ensure that support is available through some third party if participants find the interview distressing. In a current study of abused women being conducted by one of my students, she indicated in the consent that the counseling staff of a women's shelter had agreed to provide support for study participants if they found the interview process distressing. In my studies with cancer patients, my colleagues in the psychosocial department of our local cancer center have agreed to provide support for individuals who find the interview distressing. Although for the past twenty years I have been interviewing very ill individuals, many in the last weeks of their lives, no participants have requested additional emotional support or appeared to become distressed as a result of participating in an interview. Corbin and Morse (2003) note that evidence that participants find the interview process distressing is rare, and in fact participants are more likely to find the interview process helpful, which fits with my experience as well. Corbin and Morse add that participants likely manage the issue of distress in the context of an interview by simply choosing to not talk about aspects of their story that they find too distressing. For this reason, the interviewer should simply listen to the story participants provide and resist the temptation to ask such questions as "How did you feel about that?"

When coming to topics in an interview that the participant might find difficult to discuss, I generally begin by saying, "Based on what you have told me so far, I have some additional questions that might be difficult to discuss. If you would rather not talk about them, please say so." I have found that this approach accomplishes two important objectives. First, it emphasizes that the participant is in control of the topics discussed. Second, it gives the participant a few moments to "get ready" emotionally to discuss sensitive material if they wish to do so.

The decision to share information that is difficult to discuss may be accompanied by tears, pauses, or sighs. The interviewer must be ready for such possibilities and be prepared to sit quietly for whatever period of time is required for the participant to move through this phase of the interview. When the interviewer anticipates that this kind of information is likely to surface, a private setting should be available for the interview. Each interview setting is different, and some are more difficult to control than others, but when possible, researchers are encouraged to set up the space with items such as a package of tissues and some water that they can offer the participant if needed. If the participant begins to cry, the interviewer is encouraged to just sit quietly for a few minutes and then suggest a short break from the interview. In my experience, some participants who become emotionally upset during an interview appreciate the chance to take a break, whereas others prefer to continue with no break. The main point here is that the researchers should be sensitive to the needs of the participant and plan their data gathering accordingly.

Language

Language is generally understood to be the primary symbol system through which meaning is conveyed (Spradley, 1979). For this reason, participants should be interviewed in the language they normally speak. When the researcher does not speak the language of the participants, he or she must set up strategies that allow the researcher to understand the essence of what the participants said. A critical step in this process is to ensure that any individuals hired to assist the researcher are fully competent in both the language of the researcher and the language of the participant (Squires, 2008).

There are many ways in which researchers can meet the challenges of obtaining interviews in a language they do not speak. For example, in their study of the birth experiences of immigrant women from various countries, Almalik, Kiger, and Tucker (2010) were fluent in some of the languages required but trained lay volunteers to act as interpreters during interviews in languages not spoken by the interviewer. When professional translators checked the translations the lay interpreters provided, a small but significant number of errors were found. Almalik and colleagues stress the importance of developing ways to check translations, since errors at this stage in the research threaten the reliability and validity of the data.

The analysis of interview data must be conducted in the language in which it is collected. This step may require the research team to provide the person who collected the interview with some additional training so that they can help with this work. Although translation of the transcript into a language spoken by the researcher before analysis would make it possible for the researcher to conduct the analysis independently, this is discouraged because of the risk of losing important meaning embedded within the language of the participants.

The growth of expertise in qualitative research around the world has made the challenges of working in multiple languages much less formidable than it would have been a decade ago, but the issues related to translation remain central. Any translated text must be assessed to ensure not only that it is technically accurate but also that it appropriately represents the meaning embedded in language. Careful records must be kept of words and phrases that are difficult to translate, and the rationale for the meaning that is eventually assigned. This is tedious work, but there is no way around it. Our team has found that having more than one person working in each language helps to spread out the work and make such projects more manageable (Kirshbaum et al., 2010).

Many graduate programs have succeeded in attracting students from other countries who speak languages not spoken by their faculty supervisors. If a student wishes to conduct a qualitative study in a language that is not spoken by his or her supervisor, the issues related to language become more complex, because the supervisor must teach the student to analyze data in a language that the supervisor does not understand. There are likely many strategies one could devise that would facilitate this work. With one of my recent students, the interview data were collected in Farsi, which I do not speak. To ensure that she understood how to analyze the transcripts, my student arranged to have several transcripts translated into English by a person who was professionally credentialed as a translator, using the back-translation approach (Dastjerdi, 2007). She analyzed the first transcript in Farsi, and I analyzed it in English. We compared the results of our analytic work and discussed differences with a view to identifying both areas that were rooted in language and areas that required a refinement of her analytic skills. These results were applied to the translation of the second interview, again with her working in Farsi and me working in English. We found that by the time we had jointly analyzed five interviews, we had a basic sense of the kinds of translational difficulties she was likely to face, and I was comfortable with her analytic ability. She proceeded to analyze the remaining interviews on her own, carefully noting the words and phrases that were difficult to translate and the meaning she chose to give these passages.

An important point here is that although Dastjerdi could easily have prepared the translated English transcripts, we decided that the involvement of a translator who was not associated with the study would provide a more accurate document, in terms of both the technical structure of the language and the meaning of the words. Dastjerdi was concerned that if she prepared the transcript herself, she might inadvertently insert subtle changes to the text, given her familiarity with the research questions and the purpose of the study. This decision seems simple, but it is another example of the numerous choices researches must make as they work through their project. No two researchers are likely to make the exact same decisions; hence, it is critically important that all decisions be carefully documented in the researcher's journal, along with the rationale for the decision.

Silence

Periods of silence are common in interviews. The length of the silence and its meaning may vary considerably. Researchers must therefore ensure that they know how to interpret silence. The meaning of the silence may be very simple or very complex. For example, the silence may mean that the participant is thinking. In some contexts, however, local practices dictate that the interviewer sit with the participant for long periods of silence before the onset of the interview as a way of demonstrating respect. The silence may also be disease related. For example, in her study of individuals with schizophrenia, Lorencz (1991) found that silence was sometimes related to participants' needs to stop and listen to the other voices they heard.

Concluding the Interview

Informal interviews are like ordinary conversations in that they are not planned, thus the amount of time that may be required of participants is less clear than for formal interviews. The interviewer needs to be respectful of the participant's time and,when possible, schedule a formal interview if it is clear that the conversation is going to be more lengthy than originally anticipated.

Formal interviews, whether with a group or an individual, have their own ebb and flow. The time set aside for such interviews is generally negotiated at the time that the interview is scheduled and is included in the consent. Interviewers should ensure that they follow the time limits set out with the participants and that they not extend the time for the interview without the explicit agreement of the participants.

The approaches used to conclude an interview depend a great deal on what was discussed. In the event that the material discussed was emotionally sensitive, the interviewer should use small talk and other informal strategies to help "reground" the participant. This sometimes takes time, but it is unethical to leave a participant who is upset (Corbin & Morse, 2003).

If the interview takes place in the home, a participant often asks if the interviewer would like a cup of tea or coffee. This is a very important gesture, and I always make sure I have enough time so that I can stay for a cup of tea or coffee if it is offered. Although the meaning of such an invitation may vary across the world, in North America acceptance of such an invitation is a sign of respect. In my experience, participants offered refreshments seemingly as a way to reground themselves after the interview and to restore the power relations within their home. Offering tea shows in some way that they are "in control."

I keep my audio-recording device on for 10 to 15 minutes after the interview is over. There are a couple of reasons for this. Sometimes, once the interview is formally over, participants think of something else they meant to add, or they mention something new that the interviewer realizes is really quite important to the overall study. When this happens, the interviewer should ensure that he or she has permission to include this new information as data. It is also the case, however, that participants sometimes want to say things "off the record" and are waiting to make certain comments until the audio-recording device is switched off. When this happens, the interviewer must remember that information obtained off the record is generally shared in confidence and that it cannot be included as data. One may make comments about this information in one's research journal and write personal "notes to self" about how it fits with the overall direction about the study, but should clearly mark it so that it is not incorporated into the analysis.

Field Notes and Interviews

After the interview is finished, I leave the interview setting and find a place where I can stop and privately write my field notes. Field notes may be dictated into the device on which the interview was recorded or written by hand. Always make sure that field notes are dated and the interview to which they refer is indicated. Field notes are a place where notes can be made about the context of the interview and about any other aspect of the interview that may be important to its accurate interpretation. There are no rules about what can or cannot go in a field note. Sometimes I include such things as driving instructions if the location of the interview was difficult to find or if there were other related challenges. I remember reading the field notes of one interviewer in a large study in which some participants lived in fairly remote settings. The field note said, "It's the blue house by the water tower. Bring boots. The dog is friendly." Use the field notes to also record your impressions of the interview. What went well? What would you do differently? What things do you wish you had incorporated but forgot?

Debriefing Following Interviews

Debriefing following an interview is an important step in the interview process. Debriefing may take place with participants following an interview, within a research team, with gatekeepers who have helped to facilitate a study, or with moderators of focus groups if several moderators are involved (Onwuegbuzie, Leech, & Collins, 2008).

Debriefing with Participants

Debriefing with participants generally takes place after the audio-recording device has been turned off. The intention is not to attempt a summary but to just "think aloud" about the process and talk about any related questions. An additional advantage of debriefing is that by moving away from the topic of the interview itself, the interviewer is able to help "reground" the participant.

Debriefing within the Research Team

Debriefing at regular intervals within the research team helps to build collaboration within the team. Debriefing is particularly important if team members may hear accounts of experiences they find distressing in the course of the interview process. Interviewers sometimes report that a particular interview "haunts" them. This distress may be rooted in differences between the beliefs and values of the interviewer and the participant or simply a reflection of the immense difficulties and suffering faced by the participant. Although there is a growing body of literature about how to support the participant who may become emotionally upset as a result of participating in an interview, very little is written about the researcher who experiences distress as a result of the data he or she is collecting (Lalor, Begley, & Devane, 2006). Dickson-Swift, James, Kippen, and Liamputtong (2009) argue that because emotions are part of being human, the researcher should not be surprised when emotions arise in the context of research. They also acknowledge the difficulty of managing emotions in a culture that views emotions as anathema to all things scientific.

Several strategies may be used to support researchers who have strong emotional reactions stemming from the interviews in which they participate. The first of these is the research journal. I strongly encourage all my students to begin a research journal from the earliest days of their project. Daily entries provide an opportunity to write about all aspects of the research experience and to see emotion in the context of the whole study. Journaling provides a private space to explore one's own thoughts, including possible triggers for emotional responses, and their influences on subsequent phases of the research process.

Because of the potential for strong emotional reactions, individuals who are planning to conduct interviews that may be emotionally charged are strongly advised to work in research teams rather than alone. In preparation for such studies, the principal investigator is strongly advised to provide training for all team members, including those who will be transcribing the data, about how to manage the emotions they may experience.

Once the study is underway, regular meetings of the research team provide opportunities for all team members to discuss their emotional reactions during in the data generation process. Such meetings also provide an opportunity to remind all team members of the requirements related to anonymity and confidentiality with respect to the data, and the importance of not discussing the data outside the research team, regardless of its emotional content.

The principal investigator has primary responsibility for supporting members of the research team who have strong emotional reactions during the course of a study. Although it is easy to understand that individuals directly involved in the interview process may experience distress, particularly if they are young or inexperienced, the principal investigator should also remember that other members, such as the transcribers, might also find the data distressing and may require support.

Concluding the Interview Relationship

The relationships between interviewers and study participants are often very meaningful to both parties. As a result, it may be is hard to know what to do about this relationship when the study is finished. Many factors can complicate this decision, including a shared enjoyment of the discussions that arose during the study or a sense that although the study is "over" in terms of funding and the end date on the ethics application, it does not feel "finished" in terms of its original mandate. From the standpoint of the participant, the study also possibly provided an opportunity for social interaction that would otherwise have been difficult to obtain. If the interviewer and a study participant decide to continue their relationship after the study concludes, they should carefully explore the reasons for their decision and make sure that the primary motivator is not simply the reluctance to say good-bye.

In most cases, however, the relationships between interviewers and study participants do end when the study is over, and the interviewer must consider how to bring this about. The end of a qualitative study is difficult to predict, because one may wish to schedule follow-up visits to clarify some points in the analysis, even toward the end of the study. Nevertheless, at the very beginning of the project, before the consent is signed, one should give study participants the end date on the ethics application as the date when the study will officially end. On occasion, I have had to request an extension of my ethics approval and hence the period of time during which I was gathering data, but I have negotiated those instances individually with study participants. When it seems that I have gathered most, if not all, data from a given participant, my practice is to thank them personally for their contribution to my study and to follow up, where possible, with a thank you note. At this point, I sometime include a one-page summary of the main results. The conclusion of each interview relationship needs to be negotiated individually, with the primary purpose being an opportunity to convey respect and a profound sense of gratitude for the participant's willingness to share his or her experiences.

Summary

The logistical issues related to obtaining good interview data seem endless. Several of the key issues have been outlined in this chapter, but researchers are encouraged to generate their own lists of logistical issues, along with solutions for how to manage them. By tracking these solutions over time, and writing about both successes and failures, significant methodological progress can be made.

Exercises

1. Make a list of the logistical considerations that you think may influence the interview modes you will use in your study.
2. Design a small interview and conduct it in person and over the phone. What similarities and differences do you notice?
3. Are there likely to be any safety issues in your study? If so, how do you plan to manage them?
4. If you plan to generate some data in a language you do not speak, how will you manage the translation issues?
5. Do you think the individuals in your research team will find the data distressing in any way? If so, how do you plan to prepare them for the data generation experience?
6. How do you plan to conclude the relationships you develop with your study participants?

5. Transforming, Managing, and Analyzing Interview Data

O nce the interview is completed, the researcher needs to transform the interview into data. Once the interview has been transformed into data, the data need to be managed and analyzed. In this chapter I discuss two key steps in this transformational process, recording and transcribing, and provide some general guiding principles about how to manage and analyze interview data.

Recording the Interview

The researcher needs to make two main decisions related to interview recording: first, whether to use technology to record the interviews, and second, the best way to record the interview if a technological approach is being used. In the early days of qualitative research, interviews were recorded by note taking. This was primarily due to factors such as personal preference and the costs associated with the technology required. There are still some situations today in which the use of technology to record interviews would be considered inappropriate for reasons rooted in the beliefs and values of the participants. In general, however, most qualitative researchers prefer to record their interviews using audio or video technology so that they can obtain a transcript, which can then be used to facilitate analysis. The type of technology used will depend on the mode of data collection. The best strategy for recording face-to-face interviews, for example, may not work well with phone interviews. If the interviewer is planning on recording an interview, he or she must ensure that the participant understands this point fully. The use of recording technology helps to ensure that the data are as complete as possible.

The availability of digital recording devices means that files can be easily uploaded to the computer for transcription, management, and analysis. The size of the digital audio files is sufficiently small that they can easily be e-mailed to a transcriptionist if the researcher is not transcribing the interviews. Most digital recording devices include a jack for the addition of an external microphone to improve sound quality. The use of an external microphone is not always necessary, however, and the researcher should test the recording equipment in several settings to determine the best approach for obtaining a high-quality recording. Recording technology changes rapidly, and thus researchers should review available options each time they plan a study to ensure they are taking advantage of any new developments.

Following the recording of an interview, label the tape or file immediately and listen to it as soon as possible to make sure that the interview was indeed recorded. Make a copy of the recording and store it in a secure location, especially if the recording is going to be sent away for transcription. There are few things more frustrating to qualitative researchers than a lost recording.

Transcribing the Interview

If the interview has been recorded using audio or video technology, the next step in the research process is to create a transcript to facilitate analysis. Qualitative researchers rely heavily on transcripts, yet there is relatively little discussion in the literature about the issues one must consider when preparing a transcript. (For an excellent review of the literature on transcription, see a recent paper by Davidson [2009].)

The creation of a transcript is not as straightforward as it may seem. Ochs (1979) noted more than thirty years ago that transcription is theoretical in nature, with numerous decision points throughout that are closely tied to the purpose of the study. Contrary to the views of Rosenblatt (2001), Hammersley (2010) argues that although such decisions clearly result in a "constructed" text, it is also the case that transcripts comprise "more or less" the words that were, in fact, spoken, and thus, despite their "construction," one should not consider either the interview or the text resulting from the interview as fictitious or "made up."

The preparation of a transcript requires the researcher to decide whether to personally transcribe the interviews or to have them transcribed by some other person. Although the transcription of one's own interviews is time consuming, it also increases the researcher's reflexivity and the trustworthiness of the transcript (Alcock and Iphofen, 2007). Always on the lookout for ways to make it possible to transcribe interviews themselves, some researchers are beginning to use voice recognition software (VRS) programs that turn spoken words into text. These programs have improved considerably over the past two decades and now can recognize more than once voice, but some time and effort is still required to train the software for this task (Matheson, 2007).

Having the interview transcribed by someone else is less time consuming for the researcher, but it presents other challenges. For example, the researcher must ensure that the transcriptionist is properly trained and understands his or her responsibilities in terms of data confidentiality (Tilley & Powick, 2002).

Regardless of who prepares them, the researcher must decide the format for the transcripts. Should every word be transcribed? Should every pause be noted? There are two main types of transcripts. Denaturalized transcripts include every "um" and "uh," whereas naturalized transcripts employ literary conventions to increase the readability of the text (Bucholtz, 2000). Denaturalized transcripts may be more appropriate for studies based on designs such as grounded theory, whereas naturalized transcripts may be more suited to conversational analysis, and thus researchers are advised to think carefully about the kind of transcript they will require when planning the transcription of their interviews (Oliver, Serovich, & Mason, 2005).

Regardless of whether a naturalized or denaturalized transcript is prepared, the researcher must develop conventions for how to record features of speech such as volume and tone, pauses, interruption, and grammatical errors as well as punctuation. Punctuation errors can be critical; even a misplaced comma can change the meaning of a sentence (Truss, 2003).

Scholars working with certain designs, such as such as conversational analysis, have developed standard transcription formats that are widely used, but the transcription formats used in other designs may be quite variable. The transcription format need not be complicated. One easy approach is simply to write "(pause)" or to type ellipses [...] when pauses occur, to write "(unclear)" when the transcriptionist cannot make out the words used, and to write "(interrupted)" to indicate when one speaker interrupts the other.

The researcher must also decide how to indicate who is speaking within the transcript. One approach is to insert a hard return between speakers and at the beginning of each speaker's comments insert an "I:" if the interviewer is speaking or a "P:" if the participant is speaking. If the researcher is planning to use a software program for data management, he or she should check the software's format-related requirements before finalizing the format of the transcripts. If the transcript is going to be prepared by a transcriptionist, he or she must be carefully briefed on all the format decisions.

The transcriber prepares the transcript by listening to short segments of the audio or video recording and then typing what was said. This process is repeated as often as necessary to create a transcript of the whole interview. Carefully label each transcript with the participant's study number, the date the interview was conducted, the name of the interviewer, and the location of the interview (Participant 1, Nov. 29, 2010, Interviewed by Joe Smith at the participant's home). It takes roughly 4 hours for an experienced transcriptionist to transcribe a 1-hour interview and might take longer if the participant does not speak clearly or if the transcriber is inexperienced. The cost of preparing transcripts therefore may be substantial and must be kept in mind when one is planning the budget for a qualitative study that will include interviews.

After the transcript has been prepared, the person who conducted the interview must review it for accuracy. This is done by reading the transcript and listening to it at the same time. Place a notation in the footer of the transcript to indicate the date on which the interview was reviewed and the name of the person who completed this work. Interviews should not be analyzed until they have been reviewed.

In addition to correcting errors in the transcription, one may use the review of the transcript to add in any notes about the context or paralinguistic features of speech such as tone, pacing, and volume. These elements of speech are important because they aid interpretation.

I recall two cartoons that help to reinforce the importance of considering context and the paralinguistic features of speech. In the first one, a man was preparing a note for coworkers. He said, "Hello everyone, I am sitting here by the pool enjoying a cool drink." One might imagine that he was on vacation at some exotic location, but the cartoon showed his context: he was sitting in his backyard in a lawnchair watching his children playing in a small inflatable swimming pool and had a cool drink in his hand. His words alone did not convey what was actually happening and could have easily been misunderstood without additional information about his context.

The second cartoon was cleverly drawn such that the text boxes showing the comments of the speakers were created in various ways. For example, one text box looked as if it had icicles hanging from the bottom of it, while another text box had flames shooting out of it. One of the characters in the comic strip asked the other character what the meaning of the unusual text boxes was, to which the first character replied, "Oh, I am just practicing my nuances." Each researcher must find ways to capture such nuances in the interview transcript so that as much information as possible is available during the analysis.

The paralinguistic features of speech should not be ignored, because they can shed light on important aspects of the interview that would otherwise be missed; the researcher must keep track of them. For example, in our study of fatigue, both nurses and family members said that our study participants spoke more slowly when they were fatigued. Referring to this information, we compared the rates of speech of our fatigued and nonfatigued participants and found that those who reported fatigue did indeed speak more slowly. The fatigued participants also used words with fewer syllables, included fewer words per sentence, and had longer pauses between sentences than did individuals who were not fatigued. In our clinical work, we have used this additional information to help us identify individuals who may be fatigued.

Even if a researcher pays careful attention to the preceding points, the transcript cannot capture all nonverbal aspects of the interview such as head nods, smiles and other facial expressions, coughs, laughing, and emphasized words (Poland, 2001). Because these elements of communication play an important role in conveying meaning, the researcher must remember that the transcript, regardless of its format, is at best a representation of the words that were spoken during the interview.

There are differences of opinion about whether participants should be asked to review transcripts before analysis. In my experience, this strategy is not helpful, because the participants tend to spend time on correcting sentence structure and grammar and providing analytic comments about their statements rather than on helping to determine whether the transcript accurately shows what was said. Nevertheless, member checking of transcripts may be warranted in certain situations, particularly in work with sensitive information.

Managing Interview Data

Regardless of whether one has notes or a transcript from an interview, the next step is to think about how to manage the data. Interviews generate a vast amount of data: the transcript of the interview, field notes, reflexive journal notes, memos, and notes of team meetings. Unless the researcher has a plan for how all of these data will be managed before the study begins, he or she will quickly find that a systematic approach to data analysis becomes difficult. In the following sections, I incorporate strategies for managing data "by hand." These strategies can easily be moved into a software-based approach, if desired, using the conventions and techniques provided by the software developer.

After trying many data-management approaches, I have adopted the colored-paper-and-binder approach. Before beginning to analyze an interview, I purchase four colors of unlined colored paper (green, pink, blue, and yellow, for example) and a 3-inch three-ring binder, and locate my three-hole punch and some sharp pencils. I use one paper color (green) for all field notes, the second paper color (pink) for reflexive journal notes, the third paper color (blue) for memos, and the fourth color (yellow) for notes of research team meetings. I print off each transcript, as described earlier, with a 3-inch margin on the right side and with the line-number function turned on, punch holes in the transcript, and put the transcript in the binder. I put the reflexive journal notes and the field notes at the end of each interview, and the team meeting notes at the front of the binder. Memos are inserted in between the pages of the interview so that they are closest to the passage to which they refer.

Analyzing Interview Data

The early phases of the analytic process are the same regardless of the design used for the study. If the interview is going to be analyzed by hand, the researcher may wish to double-space the transcript and format it with a 3-inch margin on the right side so that there is space for handwritten notes. One may also wish to number each page and to turn on the line-numbering function so that it is easier to identify passages about which memos are written.

Every researcher develops ways to being the analysis, with the goal of getting a general idea about the main ideas discussed. The approach outlined here is one that I have personally found helpful and found easy to teach to students. Begin by reading the interview through a couple of times and then go back and draw a line across the page to mark the places where the topic of conversation shifts. This essentially separates the data into paragraphs. In the right-hand margin, make a note to indicate the topic of conversation in each paragraph. Now go back to each paragraph and consider each sentence. Circle the words that seem important given your research question. These are *in vivo* codes, named this way because they are the words spoken by the participants. In the margin I make a note about the connections between these circled words, my research question.

In general I prefer to build my analysis using *in vivo* codes, but sometimes I may add a code in the margin, using my own words to describe something I see in the data. It doesn't take long before I realize that I want to write some more detailed thoughts about the material I am reading. Sometimes these are notes to myself about a paper on a similar topic that I want to be sure to integrate. At other times, the notes are ideas about the meaning of the participant's comments. These detailed thoughts are the essence of memos. I write all my memos on the same color of paper and punch holes in the paper so I can insert the memo in my binder nearest to the page in the interview to which the passage refers.

Remember to date the memos, because memos are part of the audit trail. I also add the interview number and the location in the interview (page number and line number) of the section of text about which I am making a memo. The availability of this information helps me see how my thinking about the data is changing over time. The value of carefully labeling all memos is that at any point in the study, it is easy to pull all the memos out of the binder for review and then get them back in the right place.

It is difficult to show an example of the steps outlined above in a book, but to give a general example I have included some hypothetical text in Table 5.1, have numbered the lines, and have added some initial thoughts about some *in vivo* codes, shown as bolded words or phrases.

Here are my hypothetical field notes:

This 67 year-old man (Mr. P) was diagnosed with cancer of the oral cavity 6 weeks ago. He says he is about 6 feet tall. His normal weight is 185 lbs., but he currently weights 170 lbs. His tumor was removed surgically, and he is being treated with radiotherapy now. He is about halfway through his treatment. Mr. P was a judge for many years but retired two years ago. He lives with his wife in an apartment downtown. They have 2 grown sons, both lawyers, who live nearby with their families. Mr. P and his wife were planning on an extensive world tour and so he went to the dentist for a checkup. The dentist noticed the tumor and suggested that he follow up on it before he went away. Mr. P's prognosis is excellent, so he is still planning the tour but will wait until his treatment is over and he is feeling better. His wife is very

Table 5.1
Hypothetical Interview with Individual Being Treated for Cancer of Oral Cavity

Participant 1, Interview 1, Dec. 17, 2010	
Interview Text	**Initial Thoughts**
1 I: Thank you for meeting with me today. As you	
2 may know many people receiving treatment for	
3 cancers of the head and neck find it difficult to	
4 eat during treatment. We are interested in learning	
5 more about how we can help people eat while in	
6 treatment and resume eating as normally as	
7 possible once their treatment is finished. How has	
8 eating been going for you?	
9 P: Not very good.	
10 I: Not very good?	
11 P: Well, my **mouth really hurts**. I am **hungry**	Pain
12 **and want to eat** but I just **can't get things**	Appetite good
13 **down. I tried things I like, like pudding and ice**	Trouble swallowing
14 **cream** but you still have to put things in your mouth,	Comfort food?
15 and it just **hurts too much. Eating is so much**	Pain
16 **work**. It just **tires me right out**. Some days it's even	Eating and fatigue
17 **hard to swallow water.** My wife says I'm	Dehydrated?
18 **shriveling up.** Plus there is a **terrible taste** in my	Weight loss, dehydration?
19 mouth. What is that from? I have **lost about 15 lbs**	Radiotherapy? Infection?

Table 5.1
Continued

20	in the last month, but I was trying to lose weight so	Weight loss, not worried
21	that part is ok, but if I can't start eating I will lose	
22	more weight. **You have to eat to get better** so I am	Value of eating
23	**not sure what is going to happen.**	Uncertainty
24	I: I'd like to know more about the pain. Does it	
25	always hurt?	
26	P: Well the doctor gave me some painkillers that are	
27	pretty strong so it **doesn't always hurt but I think**	Medication helps
28	**it probably would if I didn't take the pills.** They	
29	are little but they are still **hard to swallow.** The	Hard to swallow
30	doctor said I should take them every 4 hours but I'd	
31	**rather take them before meals so I can at least eat**	Meds a strategy for eating
32	**a little. I don't like taking pills though.** I'm **afraid**	Decision making
33	**I'll get hooked on them.**	Worries about addiction

supportive and spends hours on the Internet trying to find things she could make for him to eat.

From the *in vivo* codes and my field notes I might write the following memo:

My participant is hungry but is having trouble eating (lines 11–13). The pain in his mouth and throat interfere with his ability to swallow (lines 11, 15). At time, he can't even swallow water (line 17). He links his inability to eat to some weight loss. He doesn't seem too worried about the weight loss, but there is some tension there because he notes that his wife says he is shriveling and he also links the ability to eat to "get better" (line 22). Not sure what the cause of the taste changes is or what role it is playing in his eating and drinking difficulty (line 18); need to follow up on that more in the next interview.

I might make a note such as this below in my reflective journal pages at the end of the interview:

I can't imagine being hungry but not being able to eat or drink because of pain. I would be worried that I wouldn't be able to get better if I couldn't eat and this participant seems to have similar thoughts. I don't know what to think about the weight loss. His BMI is good, but if he can't eat, he will drop below 20 quickly. People die of malnutrition and dehydration.

From this point onward, the subsequent analytic steps are heavily influenced by the research question and hence the design. If the research question were focused on decisions related to eating, and therefore the researcher is likely using a grounded theory approach, he or she may begin to group codes into categories, label the categories, begin to write about the properties of the categories, and propose relationships among the categories. In the passage provided in Table 5.1, there is information related to the relationship between a variety of symptoms (pain, difficulty swallowing, taste changes, appetite, weight loss, anxiety), eating, and drinking. Pain seems to be pivotal in relation to the decision about whether eating and drinking are possible. Despite the directions regarding medication administration provided by his physician, the participant has discovered that if he takes his pain medication before mealtime, he can eat a little more than otherwise. He also hints at trying to find things he likes to eat, such as pudding and ice cream. Thus, one could construct a category called "managing pain" and group all the codes related to pain and its management here. These codes would include those related to medication as well as food choices. In the passage in Table 5.1, one also sees some possible anxiety relating to the inability to eat. One could thus construct a second category called "worrying." Some codes, such as "rather take them before meals so I can at least eat a little," could be included in both the "managing pain" and the "worrying" categories. Including codes in more than one category is a common practice in qualitative research. This is a very useful strategy, because it helps the researcher begin to see the relationships between ideas in the data.

If the research question were focused on beliefs and values that shaped eating, one's attention would be drawn more to comments such as the link between eating and "getting better" and the tension between the usefulness of pain medication and worries about becoming "hooked." The researcher might then write a field note about the roots of these ideas in the society in which the participant lives.

When interviews are obtained from a focus group, one must also analyze the social interactions that take place. There are many approaches for doing so, but Halkier (2010) presents four options she used in a study of cooking among Danish women. She used interaction analysis, as developed by Goffman (1959), to show how self-narratives were sustained and how social relations were created within the group. She also used principles of conversational analysis based on the work of Garfinkel (1967) to examine how norms were negotiated. Halkier also used analytic strategies arising from the work of Potter (1996) in discourse psychology to examine how participants managed conflicts that arose during assigned group tasks. Last, she used positioning theory to examine how participants established their position within the group. I have applied some of these strategies under the comments column of the excerpt of a hypothetical focus group in the Appendix.

Regardless of the design used, the objective of the analytic phase is to sift through all the data—the transcripts, the field notes, the memos, and the notes from team meetings—and to use the links that run through these data sources to construct an answer to the research question.

Summary

The strategies for transforming (recording and transcribing), managing, and analyzing interviews are a central part of qualitative research. All these components must be planned carefully. One must remember that in addition to the interview transcript, other data sources related to the interview include the field notes and the memos. All these data sources must be considered carefully. Yet, no matter how attentive the researcher is to this process, he or she must remember that the data are still only representations of what was said during interview.

Exercises

1. How do you plan to record your interviews?
2. If you plan to record interviews using audio or video technology, what equipment do you plan to use? Why?

3. Do you plan to transcribe interviews yourself or to have them transcribed by another person? What are the pros and cons of personally transcribing the interviews?

4. How do you plan to manage your data? If you are planning to use software, which program will you use? Why? What steps will you take to learn how to use the software?

5. Practice coding by selecting an article from the newspaper. Draw lines to separate the paragraphs, and then circle the words in each sentence that you think are the main words that tie the sentence to the title of the article. Try to create a category that encompasses several of your codes and then write a few sentences about the category.

6. Ethical Issues in Interviewing

In this chapter I begin by returning to the concept of vulnerability, which I introduced earlier, and expand its meaning based on the work of Fisher (2006). I then provide an overview of the consent process and address the special issues related to consent that must be considered when planning to conduct a qualitative study that includes interviews. In the second part of the chapter, I discuss potential tensions between the boundaries around the research study and the boundaries around other roles the researcher may have based on his or her discipline or profession.

Research Vulnerability

In Chapter 1 I introduced the concept of vulnerability by discussing the definition developed by Chambers (1983). Chambers's definition focused on the risk of harm due to an imbalance associated with not having sufficient resources to manage crises to which one may be exposed. Fisher (2006) challenges us to expand this definition. She argues that vulnerability in research "does not rest solely upon the physical, psychological, or social characteristics that society views as disadvantageous, but upon the degree to which an individual's welfare is dependent upon the specific actions of scientists within a specific experimental context" (para. 10). The main point here is that the researcher must be fully aware that by studying individuals who are vulnerable from the standpoint of society, special safeguards must be implemented lest the researcher inadvertently increase the participants' vulnerability. For example, Fisher notes that individuals who have had limited opportunities for independent decisionmaking or for whom acquiescence to authority has become a key to survival may be more susceptible to exploitation in a research setting. She also notes, however, that relationships between researchers, individuals from vulnerable groups, and others in society such as family members and legal guardians have the potential to reduce the vulnerability of a research participant.

Fisher (2006) adds that because the harm that occurs in research settings is unanticipated, it behooves the researcher to develop strategies for ongoing monitoring of study participants that are thorough without being paternalistic. How would one recognize harm if it developed? This is not an easy question. The task of the researcher is to design his or her study in ways that minimize harm as much as possible, but it is also incumbent on the researcher to know how to recognize harm if it occurs during a study and not to simply assume that harm is unlikely. Fisher challenges researchers to recognize their moral responsibility to research participants if harm is experienced by virtue of participating in a study, including changing the research protocol even after the study is underway. The basic principle here is that the needs of the research participant must take precedence over the goals of the research. From this perspective, interviews are an opportunity to engage respectfully with individuals whose knowledge is important and valuable, with an overall objective of advancing the common good. Denzin (2001) noted that such an interview "helps us create dialogic relationships with that community. These relationships, in turn, allow us to enact an ethic of care and empowerment" (p. 43).

Vulnerability, Recruitment, and Consent

The way one thinks about vulnerability has implications for how potential participants are identified, advised about a study, and engaged throughout a study.

Recruitment

Following from the work of Fisher (2006) and Denzin (2001), recruitment must be structured so that the researcher's access to personal information about potential participants is limited until they have provided permission for access. In settings such as health care agencies and schools, this usually means that the researcher must engage the assistance of someone with access to potential participants who is willing to help identify individuals who may be interested in hearing more about the study and thus gives permission, oral or written, for the researcher to contact him or her.

Consent

Essentially all research requires that individuals be asked whether they are willing to participate in a study before information about them is, in fact, obtained. In most cases, individuals indicate their willingness to participate by signing a consent form, but in select cases, consent may be obtained orally. In a limited number of cases, such as surveys, consent is implied if an individual takes part in the survey. In past times, researchers sometimes obtained permission to conduct research without consent, but this practice is no longer permitted.

The procedures for obtaining consent vary by jurisdiction, and the researcher is advised to learn about these requirements when planning a study. Researchers should note that they are sometimes required to meet several sets of consent requirements. For example, there may be national consent requirements, requirements specified by the agency from which participants would be recruited, and requirements specified by the employer of the researcher.

The documents for obtaining consent vary by jurisdiction, with some jurisdictions requiring the inclusion of specific sections, words, and phrases. In general, the researcher is required to prepare an information letter and a consent form. The preparation of thèse two documents is time consuming. If the research is being conducted with individuals who speak some other language, the researcher is encouraged to work with a certified translator and use a back-translation approach to increase the likelihood that the meaning of the original documents is represented appropriately and in a manner that is grammatically correct. The components of the information letter outline the details of the study. The information letter may outline such topics as:

- the title of the study;
- the funder of the study;
- the names of the researchers conducting the study and the phone number for the person to call with any questions;
- the reason the study is needed;
- the purpose of the study;
- the activities that would be required if one decided to take part;
- the amount of time participation would require;
- any anticipated harms or benefits;
- the right of participants to withdraw at any point in the study with no questions asked;
- a description of how information provided would be handled to ensure that the participant could not be identified in presentations of the findings;

- a list of people who would have access to the information obtained during the study;
- the length of time the information would be kept following the study;
- a list of any costs associated with participation;
- a description of any compensation that would be provided.

For studies with ill individuals, some jurisdictions required that potential participants be told that the study is not part of standard care and that the decision about whether to participate will not have any bearing on the care they receive. Similarly, some jurisdictions require researchers working in educational settings to inform participants that the study is not part of curriculum and that the decision to participate will not have any influence on the participant's grades.

The consent form often comprises a set of statements drawn from the information letter about points such as the purpose of the study, the right to have any questions answered, and the right to withdraw at any time with no questions asked. Individuals wishing to take part in a study are asked to sign the consent form. Some jurisdictions also require that the consent form be witnessed and that the researcher also signs it. The agency from which the participant was recruited may require a copy of the signed consent form. For example, in most health care settings, a copy of the consent form is placed in the participant's medical record.

One of the fundamental issues related to the consent process is ensuring that the participant understands what the study will require of him or her. The preparation of the information letter and any other recruitment materials, such as posters and the consent form, must use simple language. Strategies for simplifying the language include limiting the use of words with more than two syllables unless they are defined, keeping sentences short, and writing using the active rather than passive voice.

Each jurisdiction usually has specific requirements for studies involving children (usually less than 18 years of age). If a child is old enough to understand the basic ideas about a study, he or she must be asked to assent to participation, and a parent must also give consent for the child to participate. In all cases, the wishes of the child take precedence over the wishes of the parent. Following from the work of Fisher (2006), several components of the consent process warrant further discussion: ongoing consent, anonymity, confidentiality, and protection from exploitation.

Ongoing Consent

In the section of the information letter outlining what the participant would be required to do if they chose to participate, the researcher must carefully outline the expected number of interviews that will be conducted. Sometimes the recruitment process requires a screening interview to confirm eligibility. If this is the case, the additional requirement for a screening interview should be included in the information letter.

Moving on to data generation, the researcher should document the interviewing mode that will be used, whether the interviews will be recorded and if so how, whether the interviews will be transcribed, and the estimated length of each interview. Because one does not know ahead of time the exact number of interviews that will be required, it is wise to indicate a range, such as one to three interviews. Participants must understand that even though they might have initially agreed to take part in a study, they are in no way obligated to continue and may withdraw at any time with no questions asked. The interviewer can facilitate this process by asking participants whether they are still willing to participate in the study when the interviewer contacts the participants for follow-up interviews. The confirmation of ongoing consent is particularly important in studies with ill individuals or others whose status might have changed between interviews.

Anonymity

It is customary in quantitative studies to tell each participant that the information provided will be confidential and that his or her identify will not be disclosed. In qualitative studies, the same provision regarding protection of identity is required. Strategies such as the removal of the names of all locations and individuals in the transcript help preserve the identity of participants, but this alone may not be enough to prevent identification, particularly if the researchers are studying individuals from a small community or group who all know one another.

The researcher should also remember that concepts such as privacy are socially constructed and that the definition used by an ethics committee may be different from the definition used by individuals or groups. For this reason, the researcher should speak informally with individuals from the population from which participants will be recruited, to ensure that the provisions for protecting the privacy of participants are acceptable. It is also the case, however, that the researcher is bound by legal requirements.

In Canada, for example, the researcher is required by law to disclose information pertaining to a threat to harm self or others. Any such legal requirements need to be clearly articulated in the information letter and discussed with potential participants during the recruitment process, as it may influence the things the participant chooses to disclose.

On occasion, individuals expressly state that they would like to be identified, but researchers are still cautioned again this unless they have explicit written consent signed by the participant giving them permission to do so.

Confidentiality

One of the most important ethical issues related to interviews is that the researcher cannot promise the participant confidentiality, because the researcher must include short passages from the transcript as evidence to support the analysis and justify the conclusions drawn. The inability to provide confidentiality must be discussed with the participants during the recruitment process. In some circumstances, particularly when the research is focused on a topic that is sensitive for social or cultural reasons, the researcher should consider discussing any excerpts selected for inclusion in publications and presentations with study participants. Sometimes participants provide information in the course of an interview to help the researcher to understand some point about their experience, but they would prefer that it not be circulated in public venues. The reflexive researcher often has a sense of the passages in the data that should be discussed with a participant to ensure permission to share them publically.

Protection from Exploitation

Researchers must carefully consider the risks and benefits to participants associated with the study they are planning. Spradley (1979) notes that exploitation occurs when the participant gains nothing in exchange for participating in the study or is harmed in some way. Eder and Fingerson (2001) add to the discussion of exploitation by noting that the researcher's desire to gain knowledge without giving something in return to the participant is an indication of the researcher's power and privilege.

There are many ways to acknowledge participants' contributions. The gains provided to participants may be simple and might include such things as a chance to help a student or to help solve a problem, but they could also be financial. The approach for acknowledging the gains should be worked out with those who know the local culture so that the researcher provides something that is meaningful to participants. The researcher must remember to include a description of whatever is provided in the ethics application when permission to conduct the study is requested and to include any associated costs in the budget if necessary. In some cases, a cash honorarium may be welcomed, but in others it might be considered insulting or coercive.

Ethical Issues Related to the Use of Interview Data for Secondary Analysis and Teaching

Researchers are often advised to consider the option of retaining data for further research and teaching purposes. Given the emphasis on the importance of concurrent data collection and analysis, qualitative researchers sometimes forget to consider the possibility that secondary analysis of interviews is also possible. To prepare for this possibility, some jurisdictions allow researchers to add a separate statement on their consent forms, requesting permission to use the data in other studies, provided ethics approval is obtained.

The opportunity to use real data in the classroom, particularly if one is teaching courses in qualitative methods, is very helpful. If the researcher would like to use the interview data for teaching purposes, a statement similar to the one for permission to conduct a secondary analysis may be required.

If permission to keep interview data for further research or teaching is not requested, the researcher must follow the requirements of the local jurisdictions regarding the period of time after which the data must be destroyed. Most jurisdictions require that data be kept for five to seven years.

Ethical Issues Related to Boundaries

Given the nature of qualitative research, interviewers who are from disciplines such as nursing, psychology, social work, and medicine that have strong therapeutic traditions sometimes experience tensions between the boundaries around the study on which they are working and the boundaries associated with their professional roles. This tension typically arises in response to information provided during the course of an interview that would normally signal a need for therapeutic intervention. The urgency of assistance required can vary. For example, a nurse interviewing a new mother could be asked for advice about feeding schedules, or an individual in a focus group could ask the moderator, who happened to be a social worker, for ideas about how to find a job. It is also possible, however, that in the course of describing his or her experience, a participant may disclose a health problem requiring more urgent attention, such as persistent pain or anxiety. Although the management of these issues is, in all likelihood, outside the boundary of the formal purpose of the study, it may be inside the boundary of the interviewer's usual role. The issue for the interviewer is how best to manage the tension between his or her roles as a research team member and as a person who has a particular set of values and skills related to his or her usual professional responsibilities. Research teams must recognize the potential for tensions between the research and professional roles of team members and develop a plan for how such tensions will be managed if they develop.

The recognition of this boundary is not an easy thing to identify, and there are different views about the interviewer's responsibility in this regard. In the case that interviews are being conducted in the context of an environment such as a community agency or health care setting, where other individuals formally hold responsibility for the therapeutic needs of the study participant, the interviewer might feel less compelled to intervene. In the community-based studies, however, where participants have been identified through such measures as a poster at a local supermarket or an advertisement in the newspaper, it is possible that the participant does not have any therapeutic support available.

When planning a study, the research team must discuss how they will manage needs for therapeutic support that arise during the course of the study, and they must be clear about this plan in their ethics application. The management plan should include the role of the interviewer and the conditions under which the participant requiring support would be withdrawn from the study. The research team may wish to consult various supports within their setting to develop their plan. For example, in our recent study of fatigue and depression (Porr, Olson, & Hegadoren, 2010), our local ethics committee was instrumental in helping our team work though the construction of a protocol for the management of psychiatric crises if we became aware of them during the course of our interviews. Our protocol included:

1. limiting participation to individuals who were under the care of a health professional;

2. before the start of the study, giving participants a one-page list of phone numbers for key community agencies that provided support in the event of a crisis;
3. withdrawing individuals from the study if they disclosed a psychiatric crisis during an interview.

Over the course of our study, we did withdraw one participant because of a psychiatric crisis. A central part of the interviewer's role was ensuring that the crisis response team was notified, as the participant was unable to do so. The crisis response team intervened and assumed responsibility for communication with the participant's health care provider. We consider ourselves very fortunate to have had these resources available and clearly understand that this might not be the case in other settings. We strongly encourage research teams to consider the potential for tensions between boundaries of the research and the professional roles of their team members, and ensure that they have a plan in place for managing these tensions if they occur.

Exercises

1. Think about vulnerability to relation to the study you plan to do. What relationships could you develop to reduce the risk of harm to the participants in your project?
2. Locate the requirements for information letters and consent forms in your jurisdiction and use them to construct a draft that includes all key requirements.
3. Determine whether there are any conflicts among the consent requirements in your county, your place of employment, and the agency from which you plan to recruit participants.
4. Think about whether you would like to keep your interview data for secondary analysis or teaching. What are the pros and cons associated your decision?
5. Do you anticipate any tensions between the research boundaries and the professional boundaries of your interviewers? If so, what plans could you put in place to manage these tensions?

7. Interviewing and Qualitative Research

Gubrium and Holstein (2001) note that society has come a long way since the days when the voice of the individual did not matter. Now society seems increasingly interested in knowing what people think, so much so that Atkinson and Silverman (1997) have suggested that we live in an interview society where every day brings new information about experiences through interviews found on talk shows and in newspapers, magazines, books, and movies.

Only a few short decades ago, the idea that interviews would also become part of the world of science would have been considered ludicrous, but given society's interest in the voice of the individual, one should not be surprised that interviews have also made their way into the research agenda. The interview is more than a way to gather information; it has become a sign of our time. Because interviews are ubiquitous, it is easy to forget that there although there are some similarities between interviews that are part of ordinary, everyday life and those that are part of research studies, there are also some important differences.

The Research Relationship

The primary feature that distinguishes everyday interviews from those that are part of research studies is rooted in the relationship between the interviewer and the research participant. The interviewer, no matter how kind, careful, and thoughtful, controls the research interview. The interview is conducted for a purpose linked to the interviewer's interest in the formal study of knowledge. The processes used in the interview are carefully prescribed in research texts, and the results have a direct bearing on the researcher's status as a scientist, and possibly on his or her livelihood. Thus, for the interviewer, there is a lot at stake in the interview process. The participants, however, have less invested in the interview. They have been asked to participate because of experiences they have had, and although these experiences have shaped who they are, the interview per se is of relatively little consequence to them.

The Research Relationship and the Interview Process

Throughout this book I have discussed the importance of recognizing the power differential between the interviewer and the participants in a study, and I have discussed its influence on the interview process, beginning with recruitment and then moving on to the generation, management, and analysis of interview data.

This power differential has implications for the ethical conduct of interviews. I have argued for the importance of maintaining a relationship between the interviewer and the participant that is characterized by respect, openness, honesty, and integrity.

The Importance of Practice

Given all the things to think about when conducting interviews as part of a research study, one can easily feel reluctant to start for fear of forgetting something or making a mistake, but there is no teacher like practice. You will learn to be a good interviewer only by interviewing. With each interview, you will learn new things about yourself and gain important insights into how the interview "worked," things you could have done to make it better, and the points where you were absolutely brilliant. Learn from your mistakes and celebrate your successes.

Appendix

Extracts from Hypothetical Interviews

Extract from Hypothetical Unstructured Interview

5 P.M., Dec. 11, 2010

Grade 3 Classroom, School 01

Interviewer: Meg Jones   Participant: T1

Transcript	Comments
I: Hello, (name). Thanks for agreeing to meet with me today. As I mentioned last week, this project is part of a larger initiative related to the professional identity of teachers. In this study I will be interviewing teachers in elementary schools. I understand that you have been here at (School 01) ever since you graduated 6 years ago. Perhaps you could begin by telling me about an average day here in your Grade 3 class.	The interviewer introduces the purpose of the interview. This is not a question per se, just an idea for a possible area of conversation.
P: Well, I leave the house at 6:30 p.m., usually get here at 7:30 so I can start setting up my room for the day. I take a break for coffee about 8:30, and then the first bell rings at 8:45 and school starts at 9. The morning ends at 11:45 for lunch,	The plan didn't work. The teacher simply lays out the chronology of the day.

and then the first bell in the afternoon is at 12:45 and classes start at 1. We go flat out until 3:30, and then that's it. By the time I clean up my room and do a few things for the next day, its 5 or so, which means I am home around 6. I: Wow! That is a long day. I bet you are exhausted. P: I am beyond exhausted. Some days I just have a glass of water and fall into bed by 7. I: I'm interested in knowing more about what you do when you are with the children. P: Well, there is a provincial curriculum that we follow. It's pretty much set in stone, but it is up to the teacher to figure out how to help the children learn the material. I love science and try to integrate science all the time, even in social studies and spelling. My kids can spell the regular Grade 3 words, but they can also spell science words of similar length. This year I got permission to develop a small module on recycling, and so the big spelling word for today was "compost." We have a worm bin, which some kids are a bit nervous about, but they love watching how those worms turn the scraps from their lunches into stuff we can put on the plants in our window boxes. We did a little experiment. We have two window boxes, but we only put the material from the worm bins on the plants in one window box. It was amazing. You could really see the difference in a couple of months. The kids were very proud of what they had discovered, and they loved bringing their parents over to show them our window boxes. They have grand plans for other things we could grow.	What was the interviewer thinking? The conversation is now off topic! Exhaustion among teachers is potentially a topic for another study. The interviewer needs to refocus the conversation and so tries to shift the conversation to what actually happens in the classroom. The teacher starts out with a technical answer. All of a sudden the teacher is excited and is having fun talking about teaching, how he designs ways to help children learn, and how he knows when the learning has happened.

Extract from Hypothetical Guided Interview

5 P.M., Dec. 11, 2010

Grade 3 Classroom, School 01

Interviewer: Meg Jones   Participant: T1

Transcript	Comments
I: Hello, (name). Thanks for agreeing to meet with me today. As I mentioned last week, this project is part of a larger initiative related to the professional identity of teachers. In this study I will be interviewing teachers in elementary schools. I understand that you have been here at (School 01) ever since you graduated 6 years ago. I've prepared some very general questions as a starting point, but please feel free to go in any direction you think that would help me understand your experience as a Grade 3 teacher. P: Sure, no problem. I: OK, so my first question is, How would you describe an average day in your classroom?	The interviewer introduces the purpose of the interview.
P: An average day? Well there really is no such thing. Every day is different, so I am not quite sure what to say.	The plan didn't work. The phrase "average day" seems to have introduced a stumbling block. He doesn't think of his day in those terms.
I: Every day is different?	Picking up on the participant's language sometimes helps participants find an anchor for their descriptions.
P: Well, we do have a set schedule in terms of subjects. For example, we have math every morning from 10:30 to 11:00, more or less. Some days the kids are really with it and we can cover a lot of material, and other days I have to do something completely different just to get	The participant was able to use the invitation to elaborate on "every day is different" to begin telling his story. Good qualitative research depends on this kind of detail.

their attention. I know that we do math every day, but I bet if you asked them, they wouldn't know that. Some days, like today, I have to sneak it in. Most of them probably think we spent half an hour talking about the hockey game, but I know we were talking about basic math skills like adding, multiplying, dividing, classifying things, different ways of grouping things, telling time, and counting backward. So I have a plan of what I want to do; some days it works great, but some days the plan is toast. You just never know (*laughs*).

APPENDIX

Excerpt from Hypothetical Semistructured Interview

5 P.M., Dec. 17, 2010

Grade 3 Classroom, School 01

Interviewer: Meg Jones   Participant: T1

Transcript	Comments
I: Hello, (name). Thanks for agreeing to meet with me again. I have a few follow-up questions, but before I start, is there anything else you would like to add from our discussion last time?	Always begin a follow-up interview with an opportunity for the participants to add any additional information they have been thinking about since the previous interview.
P: No, I don't think so. So much has happened since then. I can't remember what we talked about.	
I: No worries. One of the things we were talking about is what you do when you are in your classroom with your kids.	
P: Oh, right! We were talking about the worm bins and composting. I remember.	
I: Yes, and I was wondering: As a teacher, how do you know when your students have learned what you are trying to teach them?	Semistructured question based on previous interview
P: Ah, the million dollar question! Well I do actually have a plan in my head about this. It gets easier the more you teach. The main idea is that I want the kids to be able to put ideas together and see connections between things. Cause and effect is one of the main concepts in the Grade 3 science curriculum. The kids have to get comfortable with the idea of reasoning and with the idea that sometimes the connections they make between things will be incorrect. The trick is to distinguish between the connections that are right and those that are incorrect. I know the kids are learning when I see them trying to puzzle out the connections for themselves.	Participant easily moves to detailed description.

I: What is your role in relation to the "puzzling out"? P: Mostly to encourage and support, and help kids find information they need to solve problems, and to cheer very loudly when they are successful.	Another semistructured question.

Excerpt from Hypothetical Focus Group Interview

2 P.M., Dec. 18, 2010

Community Hall A

Moderator: Beth Wilson   Recorder: Joe Smith

Transcript	Comments
Moderator: Hello, everyone. My name is Beth Wilson, and I will be the moderator of this focus group. I would like to begin by thanking the six of you for coming out this afternoon. As I mentioned when I first told you about our study, the city administration is updating the community development plan for (Community 01) and so contracted our firm to gather some information for them. We are going to be holding four focus groups in (Community 01), and each time we will be asking similar questions. Before we start, I would like to introduce Joe Smith, who will be helping me make notes about our discussion. I will also be recording our discussion using the digital voice recorders you see on the tables, so that I can type up what was said. Having a typed version of the conversation will help me summarize the main points for the city.	The moderator states the purpose of the meeting. The moderator introduces the person recording interactions. She reminds participants of the recording and the reason for it.
Just a few things before we get started. Each of you was invited because we think you have something valuable to say. We really appreciate your participation. There are no right or wrong answers to any of the questions. Please just say what you think. We'd also like you to comment on points that other people in the group will make. Some of the people in the group may have ideas that are different from yours. We want everyone to feel welcome to say what he or she thinks,	The moderator sets the stage for the interactions. The moderator introduces the basic "rules" for the conversation.

even if they feel like their ideas are different most of the other participants. The two things we ask are that you don't interrupt one another and that you respect the views of others. You can just jump right in after someone speaks, but if you like, you can raise your hand, and I will call on you. Let's begin by just going around the table. Please say your name and how long you have lived in the neighborhood.	
(Female 1): Hi, everyone. My name is (female 1). I have lived here for 10 years. My husband and I own the house (location).	The first speaker gives additional info, the location of her home.
(Male 1): Hi, everyone. My name is (male 1). I grew up in this neighborhood and then moved away after high school. My brother and I bought our old family home on (location) 2 years ago and just moved back. Boy, have things changed!	The second speaker adds that he grew up in the community and has come "home."
(Female 2): Hi, everyone. My name is (female 2). I am from (country) and am a graduate student at the university. I just came in September. I rent a basement suite over on (location). Boy, is it ever cold here.	The third speaker adds that she is an international student and comments about the weather.
(Male 2): Well my name is (male 2). I really like (Community 01). That is why I moved here 2 years ago. I rent the apartment above (location). I don't want the city to change anything.	This participant also locates himself within the community.
(Male 3): Hi, I'm (male 3). The missus and I moved here 30 years ago, when we were first married. We built our house ourselves. It's the one (location).	This participant locates himself in community and notes how long he has been there.
(Female 3): I'm (female 3). My sister and I live (location). We love to garden and have a big vegetable garden in our backyard. We moved to that house last year, but we lived over on (location).	The participant provides the location and length of time of residence in the community. She has moved within the community.

Beth: Thanks, everyone. The first question I'd like you to discuss is, What things do you like about (Community 01)?	The moderator moves the participants to the first topic using a semistructured question informed by the information required by the city.
(Female 3): Well, I like the fact that the lots are nice and big so that we can have a big garden.	
(Male 2): And I like that the rents are low enough that I can afford to live here.	
(Female 2): Yes, that is good for me, too. The tuition for international students is so high. I was worried I would end up having to live somewhere that wasn't very nice.	Some consensus is developing here.
(Male 3): Well, you two kids seem very nice, but in the old days (Community 01) was just all people who owned their own homes—no renters. I liked it here better when there weren't any renters. People took better care of their property.	The participant introduces a different opinion of renting.
(Male 1): I know what you mean, (Male 3). That is part of what I meant by "changes" that we've seen since we lived here before.	Additional support for this different opinion.
(Female 1): Even since we moved in 10 years ago, there seem to be more renters. Is it a good thing that the rents are low? That means there could be even more renters.	(Female 1) is unsure which side of the discussion she will support.
(Male 2): What's wrong with being a renter? I am just a single guy. I work at the library, and I would love to own a house but can't imagine ever being able to make enough money to afford one, at least one here.	The participant tries to counter negative stereotypes of renting. More negative generalization to support his point of view.
(Male 3): Well, renters don't really care about the community. They haven't invested in it.	The next speaker respectfully counters with additional information.
(Male 2): I disagree. I care a lot about this community. I am a member of the community association and am on the board. I am also one of the volunteers that shovels snow for the seniors here.	
(Male 3): Well that's nice, but you don't	(Male 3) adds more information to support his point of view.

have kids, and if we don't have families with kids here, they will close the school Plus, you single young people have loud parties on the weekends.	
(Male 2): That's a pretty big generalization. I don't think I have had a party since I moved here.	Polarization is starting to develop.
Moderator: What about others in the group? Is there anything you'd like to say on this point before we move on?	Moderator steps in to manage polarization by indicating that the group will be moving soon to a new topic, but there is still a chance for any others who haven't said much to comment.
(Male 1): Well, I think renters make our community more interesting. They are from other places, like (other country), for example.	(Male 1) introduces a new idea that helps to shift the conversation.
(Male 2): Thanks, (Male 1). I like my place here. At home, we mostly just live with our families until we are married. My place is small, but it is mine.	This speaker supports (Male 1).
(Male 1): And I disagree with (Male 3) about whether renters care about the community. (Male 2) does a lot here. He even shoveled for me last winter when I had to be away. And he didn't tell you this, but he also organized the soccer program for the little kids last summer. He set it up so kids from the surrounding communities could play soccer here, even if they didn't live in (Community 01).	(Male 1) continues with new information about (Male 2) that undercuts (Male 3)'s generalizations.
(Male 3): You shovel for old people, (Male 2)? How do I get on the list?	(Male 3) moves from an entrenched position based on a generalization.

References

Alcock, J., & Iphofen, R. (2007). Computer-assisted software transcription of qualitative interviews. *Nurse Researcher, 15*(1), 16–26.

Almalik, M., Kiger, A., & Tucker, J. (2010). "What did she say? What did she say?" The impact of interpretation on recruiting and interviewing European migrant women in the United Kingdom. *International Journal of Qualitative Methods, 9*(3). Retrieved from *http://ejournals.library.ualberta.ca/index.php/IJQM/issue/view/581.*

Atkinson, P., & Silverman, D. (1997). Kundera's *Immortality*: The interview society and invention of self. *Qualitative Inquiry, 3*(3), 304–325.

Bailey, W. B. (1996). *The meaning of hope for female spouses of coronary artery bypass patients in rehabilitation.* Unpublished doctoral dissertation, St. Stephen's College, Edmonton, Alberta.

Belousov, K., Horlick-Jones, T., Bloor, M., Gilinskiy, Y., Golbert, B., Kostikovsky, Y., et al. (2007). Any port in a storm: Fieldwork difficulties in dangerous and crisis-ridden settings. *Qualitative Research, 7*(2), 155–175.

Bosio, C., Graffigna, G., & Lozza, E. (2008). Online focus groups: Toward a theory of technique. In T. Hansson (Ed.), *Handbook of digital information technologies: Innovations and ethical issues* (pp. 192–212). Hershey, PA: Idea Group.

Bucholtz, M. (2000). The politics of transcription. *Journal of Pragmatics, 32*, 1439–1465.

Carey, M. (1995). Comment: Concerns in the analysis of focus group data. *Qualitative Health Research, 5*(4), 487–495.

Chambers, R. (1983). *Rural development: Putting the last first.* Longman: London.

Charmaz, K. (2006). *Constructing grounded theory: A practical guide through qualitative analysis.* Thousand Oaks, CA: Sage.

Chiseri-Strater, E. (1996). Turning in upon ourselves: Positionality, subjectivity, and reflexivity in case study and ethnographic research. In P. Mortensen & G. E. Kirsch (Eds.), *Ethics and responsibility in qualitative studies of literacy* (pp. 115–133). Urbana, IL:NCTE.

Clarke, A. (2005). *Situational analysis: Grounded theory after the postmodern turn.* Thousand Oaks, CA: Sage.

Corbin, J., & Morse, J. (2003). The unstructured interactive interview: Issues of reciprocity and risk when dealing with sensitive topics. *Qualitative Inquiry, 9*, 335–354.

Cretchley, J., Gallois, C., Chenery, H., & Smith, A. (2010). Conversations between carers and people with schizophrenia: A qualitative analysis using Leximancer. *Qualitative Health Research, 20*(12), 1611–1628.

Dastjerdi, M. (2007). *Health care seeking practices among Persian immigrants to Canada.* Unpublished doctoral dissertation. University of Alberta, Edmonton, Canada.

Davidson, C. (2009). Transcription: Imperative for qualitative research. *International Journal for Qualitative Methods, 8*(2). Retrieved from *http://ejournals.library. ualberta.ca/index.php/IJQM/issue/view/446.*

Davis, M., Bolding, G., Hart, G., Sherr, L., & Elford, J. (2006). Reflecting on the experience of interviewing online: Perspectives from the Internet and HIV study in London. *Aids Care, 16*(8), 944–952.

Delor, F., & Hubert, M. (2000). Revisiting the concept of "vulnerability." *Social Science & Medicine, 50*, 1557–1570.

Denzin, N. (2001). The reflexive interview and a performative social science. *Qualitative Research, 1*(1), 23–46.

Dickson-Swift, V., James, E., Kippen, S., & Liamputtong, P. (2009). Researching sensitive topics: Qualitative research as emotion work. *Qualitative Research, 9*(1), 61–79.

Dowling, M. (2006). Approaches to reflexivity in qualitative research. *Nurse Researcher, 13*(3), 7–21.

Drew, S., Duncan, R., & Sawyer, S. (2010). Visual storytelling: A beneficial but challenging method for health research with young people. *Qualitative Health Research, 20*(12), 1677–1688.

Duncan, R., Drew, S., Hodgson, J., & Sawyer, S. (2009). Is my mum going to hear this? Methodological and ethical challenges in qualitative health research with young people. *Social Science & Medicine, 69*, 1691–1699.

Eder, D., & Fingerson, L. (2001). Interviewing children and adolescents. In J. Gubrium & J. Holstein (Eds.), *Handbook of interview research: Context and method* (pp. 181–201). Thousand Oaks, CA: Sage.

Eisikovits, Z., & Koren, C. (2010). Approaches to and outcomes of dyadic interview analysis. *Qualitative Health Research, 20*(12), 1642–1655.

Fetterman, D. M. (2008). Emic/etic distinction. In L. Given (Ed.),*The Sage encyclopedia of qualitative research.* Thousand Oaks, CA: Sage. Retrieved from *www.sage-ereference.com/research/Article_n130.html.*

Fisher, C. (2006). Paper three: Relational ethics and research with vulnerable populations. Online Ethics Center for Engineering6/27/2006National Academy of Engineering. Retrieved from *www.onlineethics.org/Topics/RespResearch/ResResources/nbacindex/mindex/mpaper3.aspx.*

REFERENCES

Fleitas, J. (1998). Spinning tales from the World Wide Web: Qualitative research in an electronic environment. *Qualitative Health Research, 8*(2), 283–292.

Fontana, A., & Prokos, A. (2007). *The interview: From formal to postmodern.* Walnut Creek, CA: Left Coast Press, Inc.

Frank, A. (2000). The standpoint of the storyteller. *Qualitative Health Research, 10*(3), 354–365.

Garfinkel, H. (1967).*Studies in ethnomethodology.* Englewood Cliffs, NJ: Prentice Hall.

Glaser, B. (1978). *Theoretical sensitivity.* Mill Valley, CA: Sociology Press.

Glaser, B., & Strauss, A. (1967). *The discovery of grounded theory: Strategies for qualitative researchers.* New York: Aldine.

Goffman, E. (1959). *The presentation of self in everyday life.* New York: Anchor Books.

Graffigna, G., Bosio, C., & Olson, K. (2010). How do ethics assessments frame results of comparative qualitative research? A theory of technique approach. *International Journal of Social Research Methodology, 13*(4), 341–355.

Greenfield, T., Midánik, L., & Rogers, J. (2000). Effects of telephone versus face-to-face interview modes on reports of alcohol consumption. *Addiction, 95*(20), 277–284.

Gubrium, J., & Holstein, J. (2001). From the individual interview to the interview society. In J. Gubrium & J. Holstein, J. (Eds.), *Handbook of interview research: Content and method* (pp. 3–32). Thousand Oaks, CA: Sage.

Halkier, B. (2010). Focus groups as social enactments: Integrating interaction and content in the analysis of focus group data. *Qualitative Research, 10*(1), 71–89.

Hammersley, M. (2010). Reproducing or constructing? Some questions about transcription in social research. *Qualitative Research, 10*, 553–569.

Hollander, J. (2004). The social contexts of focus groups. *Journal of Contemporary Ethnography, 33*(5), 602–637.

Kirshbaum, M., Olson, K., Graffigna, G., & Pongthavornkamol, K. (2010, May). *An ethnoscience approach to develop a cross-cultural understanding of fatigue.* Paper presented at the RCN Annual International Nursing Research Conference, The Sage Gateshead, NewcastleGateshead, United Kingdom.

Krueger, R. (2009). *Focus groups* (4th ed.). Thousand Oaks, CA: Sage.

Kvale, S. (1996). *InterViews: An introduction to qualitative research interviewing.* Thousand Oaks, CA: Sage.

Lalor, J., Begley, C., & Devane, D. (2006). Exploring painful experiences: Impact of emotional narratives on members of a qualitative research team.*Journal of Advanced Nursing, 56*(6), 607–616.

Lorencz, B. (1991). Becoming ordinary: Leaving the psychiatric hospital. In J. Morse & J. Johnson (Eds.), *The illness experience: Dimensions of suffering* (pp. 140–200). Newbury Park, CA: Sage.

Luff, D. (1999). Doing social research: Issues and dilemmas. *Sociology, 33*, 687–703.

MacDonald, K., & Greggans, A. (2008). Dealing with chaos and complexity: The reality of interviewing children and families in their own homes. *Journal of Clinical Nursing, 17*, 3123–3130.

Matheson, J. (2007). The voice transcription technique: Use of voice recognition software to transcribe digital interview data in qualitative research. *The Qualitative Report, 12*(4), 547–560.

McCoyd, J., & Schwaber-Kerson, T. (2006). Conducting intensive interviews using email: A serendipitous comparative opportunity. *Qualitative Social Work, 5*(3), 389–406.

Meier, A., Campbell, M., Carr, C., Enga, Z., James, A., Reedy, J., et al. (2006). Using the Internet to gather evidence in formative intervention research: A feasibility study of Internet "chat" focus groups in a study of lifestyle changes in colon cancer survivors. *Journal of Evidence-Based Social Work, 3*(3/4), 183–200.

Morgan, D. (1997). *Focus groups as qualitative research.* Thousand Oaks, CA: Sage.

Morris, S. (2001). Joint and individual interviewing in the context of cancer. *Qualitative Health Research, 11*(4), 553–567.

Morse, J. (2001). Using shadowed data. *Qualitative Health Research, 11*(3), 291–292.

———. (2003). Principles of mixed methods and multimethod research designs. In A. Tashakkori & C. Teddlie (Eds.), *Handbook of mixed methods in social and behavioral research* (pp. 189–208). Thousand Oaks, CA: Sage.

Morse, J., Barrett, M., Mayan, M., Olson, K., & Spiers, J. (2002). Verification strategies for establishing reliability and validity in qualitative research. *International Journal of Qualitative Methods, 1*(2). Retrieved from *www.ualberta.ca/~ijqm/1_2Final/1_2toc.html.*

Noonan, J. (2008). Ontology. In L. Given (Ed.), *The Sage encyclopedia of qualitative research methods.* Thousand Oaks, CA: Sage. Retrieved from *www.sage-ereference.com/research/Article_n298.html.*

Ochieng, B. (2010). "You know what I mean": The ethical and methodological dilemmas and challenges for Black researchers interviewing Black families. *Qualitative Health Research, 20*, 1725–1734.

Ochs, E. (1979). Transcription as theory. In E. Ochs & B. B. Schiefflin (Eds.), *Developmental pragmatics* (pp. 43–72). New York: Academic Press.

Oliver, D. G., Serovich, J. M., & Mason, T. L. (2005). Constraints and opportunities with interview transcription: Towards reflection in qualitative research. *Social Forces, 84*(2), 1273–1289.

Olson, K. (2007). A new way of thinking about fatigue: A reconceptualization. *Oncology Nursing Forum, 34*(1), 93–99.

Olson, K., Krawchuk, A., & Quddusi, T. (2007). Fatigue in individuals with advanced cancer in active treatment and palliative settings [Electronic version]. *Cancer Nursing, 30*(4), E1–10.

Olson, K., & Morse, J. (1996). Explaining breast self-examination. *Health Care for Women International, 17*(6), 587–603.

REFERENCES

Olson, K., & Morse, J. (2005). Delineating the concept of fatigue using a pragmatic utility approach. In J. Cutcliff & H. McKenna (Eds.), *The essential concepts of nursing* (pp. 141–159). Oxford, UK: Elsevier Science.

Olson, K., Tom, B., Hewitt, J., Whittingham, J., Buchanan, L., & Ganton, G. (2002). Evolving routines: Managing fatigue associated with lung and colorectal cancer. *Qualitative Health Research, 12*(5), 655–670.

Onwuegbuzie, A., Leech, N., & Collins, K. (2008). Interviewing the interpretive researcher: A method for addressing the crises of representation, legitmation, and praxis. *International Journal of Qualitative Methods, 7*(4). Retrieved from *http://ejournals.library.ualberta.ca/index.php/IJQM/issue/view/386*

Pillow, W. (2003). Confession, catharsis, or cure? Rethinking the uses of reflexivity as methodological power in qualitative research. *Qualitative Studies in Education, 16*(2), 175–196.

Poland, B. (2001). Transcription quality. In J. Gubrium & J. Holstein (Eds.), *Handbook of interview research: Context and method* (pp. 629–649). Thousand Oaks, CA: Sage.

Porr, C., Olson, K., & Hegadoren, K. (2010). Tiredness, fatigue, and exhaustion in the context of a major depressive disorder. *Qualitative Health Resaerch, 20*(10), 1315.

Potter, J. (1996). *Representing reality, Discourse, rhetoric and social construction.* London: Sage.

Rosenblatt, P. (2001). Interviewing at the border of fact and fiction. In J. Gubrium& J. Holstein (Eds.), *Handbook of interview research: Context and method* (pp. 893–909). Thousand Oaks, CA: Sage.

Sinding, C. (2010). Using institutional ethnography to understand the production of health care disparities. *Qualitative Health Research, 20*(12), 1656–1663.

Smith, D. (1996). The relations of ruling: A feminist inquiry. *Studies in Cultures, Organizations, and Societies, 2*, 171–190.

Spradley, J. (1979). *The ethnographic interview.* New York: Holt, Rinehart, and Winston.

Squires, A. (2008). Language barriers and qualitative nursing research: Methodological Considerations. *International Nursing Review, 55*, 265–273.

Stone, L. (2008). Epistemology. In L. Given (Ed.), *The Sage enclopedia of qualitative research methods.* Thousand Oaks, CA: Sage. Retrieved from *www.sage-ereference.com/research/Article_n137.html*.

Sturges, J., & Hanrahan, K. (2004). Comparing telephone and face-to-face qualitative interviewing: A research note. *Qualitative Research, 4*(1), 107–118.

Tilley, S., & Powick, K. (2002). Distance data: Transcribing other people's research tapes. *Canadian Journal of Education, 27*(2/3), 291–310.

Truss, L. (2003). *Eats, shoots and leaves.* New York: Gotham Books.

Warren, C. (2001). Qualitative interviewing. In J. Gubrium & J. Holstein (Eds.), *Handbook of interview research: Context and method* (pp. 83–101). Thousand Oaks, CA: Sage.

Wenger, G. (2001). Interviewing older people. In J. Gubrium & J. Holstein (Eds.), *Handbook of interview research: Context and method* (pp. 250–278). Thousand Oaks, CA: Sage.

Index

About the Author

Karin Olson is a Professor in the Faculty of Nursing and a Distinguished Scholar in the International Institute for Qualitative Methodology at the University of Alberta in Edmonton, Canada. Her research is focused on symptom experience in advanced cancer. She is especially interested in documenting links between behavioral and physiological processes associated with symptom experience and in developing methodological approaches for showing the social construction of symptom experience.